The Story of Strathearn

An Anthology of People and Places

by

Colin Mayall

ISBN No. 0-9541263-1-9

Published by
Jamieson and Munro

Printed by
The Monument Press, Abbey Road, Riverside, Stirling FK8 1LP

*This book has been produced by Jamieson & Munro
and production costs were supported
by a grant from the
Trustees of the John Jamieson Munro Charitable Trust*

Bibliographical Note

The author, Colin Mayall, has lived in Strathearn for some twenty years. Born in Renfrewshire he was educated at Hutchesons' Grammar School in Glasgow, the Royal College of Science and Technology (now Strathclyde University) and the College of Estate Management. He spent many of his summers staying in Crieff in the 1940s with family friends and recalls many a game of draughts in the Square on warm August afternoons! His wife, Elizabeth Sharp has family connections from Muthill and Blackford dating back to the 17th Century. After qualifying as a surveyor and working all over Scotland he spent a number of years in the Middle East before settling down in Perthshire. Married with children and grand children, he retired from his own business to pursue his fascination with genealogy and Scottish history. He set up Caledonian Connections in 1997, which has developed many links with expatriate Strathearn people all over the globe. He took a history research course through the Open University and the substance of his thesis on the weavers of Strathearn is included in this book. He has taught both genealogy and local history to further education students.

A former Chairman of Strathearn Speakers Club, he speaks regularly to Clubs, Schools and Societies on a variety of topics of local interest. For many years he has been rugby correspondent to the *Strathearn Herald* and was for some 18 years on the Committee of Crieff Rugby Club holding a number of positions including President and Secretary.

Index

Introduction

A DIFFERENT WORLD

It is said that when God created the Garden of Eden, he decided that the language could only be Gaelic. As one whose deep genealogical roots lie in the gaeldteacht, I grieve that so much of our heritage has been usurped and over written by the somewhat blasé approach of contemporary historians. I live in Strathearn, an area that causes problems to many as to exactly where it lies! Strathearn to many people is undefinable but to us, the people of the Strath, it is quite clear. The Strath is the "valley" of the River Earn. In this anthology I have used the parishes as defined within the Statistical Accounts. The what? These Accounts are a somewhat unique record of Scotland over the years, and were produced for the most part by the Ministers of the Parish. Although rather biased in approach, they did project the life style from an honest but somewhat Calvinistic point of view. Within this book, for the record I have included accounts of stories and information from the following Parishes: Balquhidder Comrie, Crieff, Monzie, Strowan and Monzievaird, Fowlis Wester, Madderty, Gask and Findo Gask, Blackford, Auchterarder, Methven, Dunning and Glendevon. I know that perhaps there is argument that I have wandered over what can rightly be regarded as pure Strathearn. I am unrepentant. These parishes in my opinion truly represent the area I consider to be perhaps "Greater Strathearn"!

There is a strange mixture within these parishes of Celtic culture and a strong Lowland presence. In Crieff in particular there was resentment to the intrusion of the Gaelic. It manifested itself when many Gaels settled in the town in the 18th and 19th centuries. The uniqueness of the situation locally was that whilst Crieff was undoubtedly a Lowland town, many of its immediate neighbours were indubitably Highland. Comrie and Monzie parishes fell into that category. It is clear that there was indeed tension between the two groups. I believe much of this feeling had been probably exacerbated by the annual arrival in Crieff of the Highland drovers and the excesses enjoyed after a long time on the drive from points north and west. Even more relevant are the diatribes delivered by the clerics against both the Jacobites, Episcopalanians and Catholics who dared corrupt the ways of the God fearing Calvinists and Hanoverians! Indeed, I believe after having read many contemporary accounts of the time that a web of biased accounting has been spotted!

I will elaborate on this later. I have called this an anthology as I have no intention of being a latter day "Porteous"! He produced a well documented book which is still regarded by many as the "bible" of Crieff's past. For the most part it provides us a vivid picture story of much of Crieff that would be forgotten. My intention is however to broaden those horizons and attempt to provide a contemporary look at Strathearn and its unique past. The various snippets are the product of years of gleaning and I trust that they will give the reader an idea what life in Strathearn is, and was. I am conscious that many of the tales related in books produced in the late 18th and early 19th centuries had a detectable historical bias. I have attempted to quote wherever feasible the prime sources of my research so that you can if you so desire pursue the quest for further knowledge!

I would like to thank the many individuals who advised me as I went along not least of all those tolerant librarians both in Crieff and in the A K Bell in Perth as well as the folk of Strathearn who shared with me the tales of their past.

I have endeavoured to present an historically accurate picture of Strathearn past and present. Where possible I have used my sources prime or otherwise. I have tapped the incredible information packed away in newspaper archives both in Crieff and in Perth. Inevitably I have referred to other publications including *The History of Crieff* by Alex Porteous, *Crieff Its Traditions and Characters* published by D Macara, *The Jacobite Rising of 1715* by John Baynes, *St Michaels Milestones 1560-1982* by the Rev Dr E S P Heavenor, *The Scottish Central Railway Perth to Stirling* by Peter Marshall (The Oakwood Press, 1998), *Crieff in the Victorian Era* by Dixon published in 1897, *Historic Scenes of Perthshire* by William Marshall of Coupar Angus (1880).

The illustrations come from a variety of sources. Let me acknowledge with grateful thanks my dear friend Joan Longden who lent me her superb post card collection of Strathearn and carte blanche to reproduce, David Ferguson for the Crieff railway station photographs, Grace Cuthbert for the etching of Inchbrakie and the enthusiastic members of Strathlearning Local History classes who acted as guinea pigs when fed with notes from the manuscript of this book!

I dedicate this work to my late son Richard P Mayall, sadly missed.

COLIN MAYALL,
Crieff, 2001.

Chapter 1

THE EARLY OCCUPANTS

The Picts - who were they ?

According to Lynch (*Scotland: A New History*; Century Ltd, 1991), the first mention of the Picts was in AD 297, the name meaning simply the painted people. Originally probably two groups of people, the Maeatae to the south and the Caledonii to the north. In the 6th century Bede differentiates between the Northern Picts and the Southern Picts, the latter having been converted to Christianity by St Ninian.

The book *Picts, Gaels and Scots* written by Dr Sally M Foster (B T Batsford Ltd/Historic Scotland, 1996) gives perhaps the best and most succinct account of the early occupants of these lands.

Classical and later historic sources use a variety of evolving terms to signify the people who inhabited Scotland and /or their territorial divisions prior to the late eighth century. Of these terms Picti, first recorded in 297 and derived from the Picts own name for themselves, or possibly a Roman nickname meaning "the painted ones", has been the most enduring. Then as in later Classical sources, the Picts were referred to as assailants of the Roman frontier in Britain. Much ink has been spilt over what the ancient writers meant by Picts, but it seems to be a generic term for people living north of the Forth-Clyde isthmus who raided the Roman Empire.

There is a distinction in archaeological remains to north and south of the Forth-Clyde isthmus in the early centuries which would seem to support this definition, although some archaeologists argue that the cultural boundary lay further north, at the River Tay. The Picts seem to have been an amalgam of earlier tribes – as many as twelve were recorded by Ptolemy (an Alexandrian geographer) in the second century. Tacitus, the Roman historian, records that some of these tribes combined against the army of his father -in-law, Agricola, in 83 AD after the battle of Mons Graupius.

There need be no suggestion that they were indeed a nation or even a uniform people, indeed at least two main internal divisions are referred to: the Maeatae and Caledones and other Picts, who had become Verturiones and Dicalydones by the mid-fourth century. We cannot even be sure that these were the sole inhabitants of the country. We also do not know the name the Picts might have used for themselves (if indeed they recognised the concept!). We can be confident that they were simply the descendants of the native Iron Age tribes of Scotland, most of whom were never part of the Roman Empire and even when they were, were only affected for short periods of time. The notion of the Picts having existed in Galloway is now recognised as a myth which arose out of a misunderstanding by mediaeval writers.

Therefore in historical terms the term Pictish might be applied to the period between 79 AD, when the Romans advanced beyond the Forth-Clyde isthmus into Caledonia, and 842/900 AD when the MacAlpin dynasty came to establish itself. In practical terms the Picts (and indeed Dal Riata) only become truly recognisable as archaeological and historical entities from the sixth century, and it is on this later period that we shall inevitably concentrate.

Territorial divisions of Pictland

Strathearn was the southern bastion of Pictland. There were seven separate kingdoms or provinces named after the seven sons of Cruithne, an early Pictish king. In the far north the lands of Caithness were called Cat, whilst south of this lay Fidach and Ce. These formed the three Northern kingdoms lying above the Mounth or what is now termed the Cairngorms or modern Deeside. The four southern kingdoms comprised Circinn or Angus, Fotlaid or Atholl, Fib or Fife and Fortren or Fortriu which encompasses the lands of Strathearn and Menteith. As these Pictlands gradually developed their identity from the northern tip of mainland Scotland down as far as what is now the start of the Lowlands, there was a simultaneous domination by the Norsemen or Vikings in the islands of Orkney, Shetland and the Western Isles. By the ninth century, Caithness or Cat was also under the domination of the warriors from across the North Sea.

In the fourth century Pictish power lay in Strathearn. By the time of the battle of Dunnichen Moss in Angus when the Picts, under Bridei mac Bile, defeated the Northumbrian invaders, Fortren was unchallenged as centre of Pictish royal power where it remained. To quote Lynch: "The growth of the kingdom of Fortren/Fortriu conveniently summarises the development of Pictish kingship. The seventh century saw the development of this tribal power into being 'overkings' of all Pictland south of the Mounth by the second half of the 7th century".

By the eighth century Forteviot was the centre of Pictish royal power. By this time there was a strong Scots influence. The Scots were based in the Kingdom of Dalriada, modern Argyll and abutted with the western part of Fortren. By the 9th century, the rulers of Fortren were of Scots rather than

Pictish descent. Oengus ll (or Unuist) ruled from Forteviot. He died in 839, the year the Vikings defeated the Picts of Fortren and two of Oengus's sons were killed thus paving way for Kenneth Mac Alpin to take over as first King of Scotland.

Regretably much of the early history of Strathearn is lost in the mists of antiquity. Apart from the obvious remains of our Pictish ancestors and their ubiquitous standing stones, some traces do exist of a civilisation prior to this. Not surprisingly many of these remains are the hill forts and settlements built on high ground above a strath or valley. These appeared in Scotland in the 8th century BC prior to the introduction and the manufacture and use of iron from the continent. North of Crieff perched above the tortuous meanderings of Wade's road, lies Dun Mor (NN 906 304) at a height of some 465 metres (1526 feet) overlooking the Glen and Lower Strathalmond. Nearby to the south was situated the Roman Fort of Fendoch described later. Dun Mor's past is not clear. It has been suggested that perhaps it was never completed. Whatever happened, alas, we are never likely to know. It was of a fair size, measuring some 150' x 90' and as was the case of the brochs found further north possibly served as a place where the local inhabitants could withdraw to in times of danger.

Callums Hill (NN 875 223) in Crieff was too probably the site of a similar communal defence or habitation. Although the creation of a small housing development in the 1960s has obscured much, a report in the Perthshire Advertiser dated June 1967 is worth recalling. *"A Bronze Age urn containing human bones was unearthed at Callum's Hill, Crieff in a pit on a building site. The area is in the neighbourhood of an Iron Age fort."*

A Pictish Miscellany

Strathearn was invaded by Egfrid of Northumbria in 685 on his way to defeat at the Battle of Nechtansmere. The Annals of Ulster and the Pictish Chronicles accounts tell of the Picts of Fortren defeating the Vikings/ Norsemen in 839. The King of Fortren was killed (Eoganan). Fortren was at that time probably under Northumbrian control after the Romans departed.

Fortren or Fortriu as a kingdom was first mentioned in 664. The Verturiones a Celtic tribe were, prior to this the inhabitants of Strathearn. In Strathearn it was the ri or tribal king who ruled. They eventually controlled all Pictland south of the Mounth. To quote Lynch "The achievement of the Kings of Fortriu in the 8th and 9th centuries was one of the most notable in Scottish history".

The Picts were descended from the tribes which occupied the area north of the Antonine wall. These were the Maeatae and further north the Caledonii. The hill fort on Sheriffmuir, Dumyat (NS 832 973) has been translated as meaning the fort (dun) of the Maeatae. It lies in a strategic spot affording extensive views over the valley of the Forth and the surrounding hills. These forts including Dundurn at St Fillans and Dunadd in Kilmartin (Argyll) are all similar. A mixture of stone and timber and often having examples of vitrification ie the stones were fused together having been subject to bonfires of wood, bracken and peat.

Mons Graupius

The Picts or Caledonians of the north were led by Calgacus and clashed with Agricola at Mons Graupius probably near Bennachie in Aberdeenshire. The Caledonians had a force estimated at 30 000 men with chariots and long swords. Their tactics were unsuited to combat the efficiency of the Romans and defeat resulted. What happened to the Maeatae? It is speculation but they possibly lived in the shadow of the Romans, not subjugated but led a somewhat strained co existence.

What is left of the Picts in Strathearn?

Language

The Picts spoke "P-Gaelic" which is unlike the Scots Gaelic of today. It is more akin to Welsh, Breton and Cornish. The Picts used an Ogham alphabet as seen on inscribed stones scattered throughout the east of Scotland. Place names indicating a Pictish presence start with "Pit" or "Pett". It means a parcel of land and is generally not found south of Antonines Wall. In Strathearn, place names still found with this prefix include Pittentian, Pittachar, Pett Farm at Muthill and Pitkellony. Other Pictish or "P-Celtic" place names are found throughout Scotland include Carden (eg Cardenden), Lanerc (eg Lanark), Pert (Perth), Pevr and Aber.

Standing Stones

In Scotland, the stone circles and alignments belong to the third millennium ie 3000 BC. This was a time of change when communal burial was replaced by individual burial and new types of pottery and metalworking were first introduced. First we find copper artefacts and then bronze. The communal burial of the people took place in stone chambered cairns or barrows. Stone circles or henges were ceremonial and often recorded celestial movement. Single stones are found all over Strathearn and are similar in size and shape to that imposing edifice in the field immediately before the Stuart/ Strathearn Crystal on the Muthill Road. These stones were possibly tribal boundary markers.

The First Millennium ie 1000 BC saw the construction in Strathearn of defended settlements and hill forts. By 200 BC, brochs had begun to appear in parts of Scotland. An example albeit outwith Strathearn, is found at Laws of Monifieth off the B961 (OS ref NO 491 349).

Standing stone above the village of Fowlis Wester. This one formed part of a stone circle dating back to probably 3000 BC.

Pictish symbols and cross slabs

These date from the mid 6th century until the mid 9th century. They are divided into three classes.

Class I: Designs which are incised not carved in relief on boulders or on rough dressed stones. No Christian crosses or other recognised attributes. Dating uncertain, possibly 7th, 8th and 9th centuries. Designs are Crescent and V-rod, the notched rectangle and Z-rod and the arch and horseshoe. Also animal forms like serpents, bulls and boars.

Class II: Found after Picts were subjugated by the Scots. Date from 9th century. Christian influence with crosses. Old symbols less pronounced. Carved in relief on one side. 9th and 10th century.

Class III: Monuments with Celtic ornament in relief but without the symbols of Classes I and II. Up to the 12th century

Pictish and older remains in Strathearn

The Picts may have gone but their remains are still very much with us. Indeed many of the older established families in and around the Strath have undoubtedly the genes of those mysterious people. Their heritage is indeed there to see. Look around and espy their physical remains!

Abernethy Round Tower: Early 11th Century. Refuge for relics and people in troubled times.

Fowlis Wester (OS ref NN 927 240): The two stones are displayed in the old kirk at Fowlis a couple of miles east of Crieff. The first is over 3 metres in height and shows a man leading a cow with a bell and two horsemen in two tiers with a beast between them. One man has a hawk on his arm. There is a man with a cow who heads a procession of six bearded men. At the bottom of the stone is a man who appears to being devoured by a beast. The second stone was found during restoration in the 1930s. It is in good condition and appears to depict Jonah and the whale. Shown also are two clerics sitting opposite one another. They could be two saints, possibly St Paul and St Anthony. The 1837 Statistical account for the Parish of Fowlis Wester refers to the existence of "Druids" referring to the stone circle above the village. To quote what was written at the time:

"Fowlis appears to have been a favourite seat of the Druids. Several of their clachans have been demolished but there are still four large Druidic stones standing west from the village one of which is a croleach or alter stone, in which there is an artificial cavity where the blood and oil of the sacrifices flowed. On the summit of the hill due north from the same place there is a Druidic circle of stones and a double concentric circle. This is believed to have been the temple of an arch Druid which when erected was probably in the midst of a forest in which were the oak and consecrated grove, the favourite objects of their superstition. The circle consists of sixteen stones between which and the double circle there is a large stone incumbent where the arch druid stood and addressed himself to those around him. The outer precinct of the concentric circle is 18 yards in circumference in which there are 40 stones. Three yards north from it there is a large standing stone which is probably monumental of some illustrious dead as they were then interred around those places, where they worshipped the Supreme Being. To the west of this temple there is a Siun which signifies in Gaelic a mount of peace, near which is a fairy hillock where urns have been found, and which is believed to have been inhabited by an inferior kind of genii called fairies. On the Siuns , the Druids held assizes when it was customary to kindle a large bonfire called Samhin or the fire of peace. On Hallows Eve, a druidical festival, these fires are still lighted up in this district and retain the same name."

The same Account later on mentions the cross and states that there were once chains where culprits were attached to and exposed to punishment like a pillory. There is a story that up until the turn of the century the old cross was smeared in grease to ward off evil spirits.

Other Pictish relics in the Strath include near **Auchterarder** (OS ref. NN 942 097): A Pictish symbol stone 2 miles SW of Auchterarder. This is a Class 1 stone and lies near the south side of the road. It is incised with a bird with its head turned back (a goose?) and a double-sided comb. **Dupplin Cross:** Not really Pictish but a "hybrid" monument of Dalriadic design by sculptors trained in the Pictish tradition. Now located in Dunning near Forteviot the old Royal Pictish capital. **Dundurn** (OS ref. NN 707 233): Located at the east end of Loch Earn at St Fillins Golf Club. A high terrace and four lower terraces enclosed by ramparts. A nuclear fort, ie an inner citadel and a series of outworks/ramparts. Dates from about AD 465 to beginning of 7th century. Rebuilt using Roman stones from a ruined fort nearby. According to Professor AL Cock's excavations there were terraced farming below the fort. Wild cherries, rasps and hazelnuts were grown and bracken was collected for bedding and litter and mosses as an equivalent of lavatory paper. Glass beads have been found. These were believed to have been imported and melted down and made into smaller beads. A barrel padlock was also found there during excavations. According to Annals of Ulster, Dundurn was under siege in 683. It is reckoned to have been utilised as a fort from about 100 BC. Rossie Law (OS ref. NN 997 124): About 2 miles SW of Dunning, this fort is the largest of those which occupy peaks on the north face of the Ochil range overlooking Strathearn from the south. Formed by a single wall measuring 14' thick in places it encloses an area 600' x 500'. Traces of timber buildings have been found. Machany (OS ref. NN 902 158): A fort some 3 miles north west of Auchterarder occupying a low ridge 400 metres north of Machany close to the right bank of Machany Water. An oval enclosure 170' x 115' within a wall now reduced to stony mound about 15' thick. There is evidence of vitrified remains.

The Picts – who were they ?

It is clear that despite the quite obvious physical remnants of our Pictish ancestors, we know little about them as a people. The following may well through a wee bit light on the mystery.

Extract from *The Rise of the Celts* (Hubert, H 1934)

Hubert was a French scholar who died in 1927. This extract is somewhat dated by modern standards but was the first real study of Celtic peoples.

"The Neolithic population had left remnants in the two islands, and, also in the two islands there had been Iberian settlers. But the racial map of Britain shows nothing corresponding to the Erainn. On the other hand, there is another group of tribes which is common to both islands; it, too, was very considerable, and in the north of Ireland it formed a mass comparable to that formed by the Erainn in the south. These were the Cruihnig. The Cruithnig are the Picts, who were a distinct people in the larger island, occupying all or part (but the chief part) of Caledonia before the Scots – that is the Irish, the Gaels – came into the country and hewed a domain for themselves out of their land. In Ireland the Picts held a large part of Ulster where they were so numerous that they became the preponderant power. In Connacht there were communities of Picts near Cruachain, the capital and there were others in Munster, Meath and Leinster. The Cruithnig of Ireland are called Picti in the Irish annals. The Caledonian Picts are called Cruithnii or Cruithini populi in Adamnan's Life of St Columba and the Irish list of the Pictish kings begins with an eponymous founder, Cruidne.

It is therefore certain that the two terms are equivalent. The Pictish people took up enough space to give its name to the whole of the British Isles. If we suppose that the c of Cruithnig represents a qu which was destined to become p in Brythonic, we can go back through the forms of the sister language to a form Qurteni (artani) or Qretani. The corresponding name for the country was pronounced Pretani in Brythonic, from which comes Welsh Prydain. Ynys Prydain is the name of the island of Britain. Pytheas heard this name about 300BC. But it is uncertain whether he heard them called by this name in Gaul or in Britain itself.

The name is intelligible in Celtic. It is generally traced back to Irish cruth, Welsh pryd, meaning 'form'. The Picts had a name among the Romans for tattooing themselves with animal and other forms.

The word Pict has no such ancient history. It is first met in a panegyric of 296 in honour of Constantius, who commanded in Britain. It is thought that it might be merely a Latin name given by the Romans, a kind of nickname afterwards consecrated by the chronicles. Caesar in his account of the Britons of the interior says that they painted themselves for war with woad. Picti Brittani Martial repeats. so the Picts would be Britons who still remained savage outside the Roman frontier. A Celtic explanation of the word has, however, been put forward. It is supposed to come from a root meaning 'to tattoo', beginning with qu which became p in Brythonic. From the same root came Irish cicht, meaning 'engraver'. The Gaullish proper names Pictllus, Pictilus, Pistillus are diminutives of a term which may have been identical with the names of the Picts and has not been preserved."

This article written by Hulbert was published in 1934 after his death.

The Post Pictish Period in Strathearn

After the initial Pictish period there was the REGNUM AND GENS (Crown and people). In this period a federal Pictish evolved by accident as much as by design into Alba, a Kingdom expressed in terms of a territory as well as of a group of people. Kings of Picts became Kings of Scots, still a collection of separate peoples.

The centre of this Kingdom still lay in Fortriu or Fortren, modern Strathearn. Scone is believed to have been the actual centre. Kings consolidated their power but localities also developed a stronger sense of their own identity. Kings of Scots emerged but so did the "mormaers" or "great stewards" in a number of regions. The kings of Scots in the 10th and early 11th centuries had less power than the earlier Picts. A surprising number of Kings met violent deaths in the North between 900 and 1058. It was a period when Scots as such were described as French, English and Scots. These two centuries form an enigmatic period starting with Kenneth Mac Alpin and ending with Macbeth.

Forteviot

Kenneth mac Alpin took over the Pictish kingdom between 839 and 844. He was a Scot of Dalriadic origin from the branch of Cenel Gabrain. Why he ended up as king is not clear. There was precedent in that Scots had occupied similar positions. He took up his kingship at Forteviot in Strathearn. The tales that emerged after his death were numerous and basically unsubstantiated. It was said that he had seized power in an illicit coup. The account of his reign in the book Berchan's Prophecy states that he purged the Pictish nobility in a single act of treachery, at perhaps the first but not the last "black dinner" in Scottish history. Extra colour was given to the story when it was stated later that traps had been set under the benches for the unsuspecting Pictish nobles. It is clear however that Kenneth has now been recognised as first King of the Scots.

During his reign he invaded Lothian six times. In turn the Britons raided as far as Dunblane whilst the Danes got as far north as Dunkeld. It was however only after his death that the regnum of the Scots moved to Forteviot. Although Kenneth claimed to be King of Scotland his rule in fact covered the southern Pictish Kingdoms of Fortren itself, Fib or Fife, Circenn and Atholl. His influence was indeed less than his Pictish predecessors, Kings of Fortren, namely Constantine and Oengus. At this time the Pictish kingdoms north of the Mounth probably moved out of his domination. He was an ambitious but somewhat unsuccessful warlord.

The Church

In 849 the relics of St Columba were moved to Dunkeld from Dalriada in the West. This is significant as he was the Patron Saint of Dalriada. Scone became the centre of Fortren and the place where Scots Kings were to be crowned. St Andrews in Fife as the name suggests was the centre of veneration for St Andrew and had been established a century earlier during the reign of Constantine.

The MacAlpin Dynasty

Ruled in the male line with one exception until the death of Malcolm II in 1034. Direct patrilinear succession (ie down the father's side) was not established in that period. Tanastic succession was the Celtic law of succession whereby the crown was passed to the strongest or most suitable male heir from the immediate family. Without exception grandsons and cousins or sometimes brothers succeeded rather than sons. Life was short. Of the 14 between the death of Kenneth in 858 and 1034, no fewer than 5 reigned for 5 years or less and a further 4 survived less than 10.

The politics of this period still involved the minor Kings of Scots and Picts as well as the Dumbarton Kings of Strathclyde. Strathclyde had become a subservient kingdom to MacAlpin's based in Strathearn. The Britons inflicted defeat upon them at Abercorn near the Forth. Another threat had arisen from the Viking Kingdom based in York. Politically Kenneth MacAlpin chose a mixture of names for his sons, Pictish, Roman, Gaelic and Scandinavian. (ie Constantine, Aed and Olaf.)

Scandinavian Threat

Kenneth Macalpin had in the 830s aligned himself with the Viking King of the Hebrides. Constantine ll married off his daughter to Olaf lll Norwegian King of Dublin as Kenneth had done before him. Viking (Danish) York was played off against Norwegian Dublin.

In 866 Olaf King of Dublin attacked and laid waste much of Pictavia. Four years later he sacked Dunbarton the Briton's capital after a 4 month siege. He attacked Galloway and the north of England, slew a Saxon King and returned to Dublin with 200 ships and countless slaves and booty.

In 869, the Pictish Chronicles record that Fortren was ravaged and plundered by the Danes who carried off hostages.

In 874 his successors laid waste the North of Scotland including Caithness, Moray Ross and Sutherland. A year later he was defeated and the lands recaptured.

In 877, Constantine was killed at a battle with the Danes in Fife. The armies clashed at Dollar.

In 889, Harold King of Norway captured the Western Isles. Orkney and Caithness come under Norwegian jarldom In 900, Danes pillaged the east coast of Scotland and Donald King of Scots was slain at Dunotter. At this time the tower at Abernethy was constructed.

In 903, the Danes again attacked Fortren but were beaten by the local men thus fulfilling the "Prophecy of St Berchan":

> *By him shall be attacked the powerful house*
> *Ah, my heart! on the banks of the Earn,*
> *Red shall be the colour of the house before him,*
> *He shall fall by the men of Fortren.*

Legend states that the Men of Fortren went into battle with the crozier of St Columba as its standard. This was the last of the attempted Scandinavian invasions of Mac Alpin's realm.

The Battle of Monzievaird

In 997 Kenneth IV came to the throne. Called Grim or Donn (brown) he fought a civil war in Strathearn with Malcolm son of the previous Kenneth lll who was king of Cumberland and laid claim to the Scottish throne. He invaded Strathearn in 1004 and the sides clashed at Monzievaird, probably on the south side of Ochtertyre. Kenneth was slain and Malcolm ll became King. The OS map (ref. NN 823 287) shows the site to the east of Loch Turret and it is called Cairn Chainachan or the cairn of Kenneth.

Ethnic Features of Early Inhabitants

In Scotland generally there are certain distinguishing features. The Celts and early settlers of Dalriada in the west (Argyll) were in general small and dark whilst those of the northern counties such as Caithness and Sutherland were taller and with a higher incidence of fair or red hair. (Scandinavian/ Viking influence).

The incidence of blood group B diminishes in Europe from East to West but in Britain its frequency rises in the North (Scotland) and the West (Wales) indicative of the Celtic occupation. Blood group O again in Wales and in Scotland have a much higher incidence than in the southern counties of England. This again is a Celtic characteristic.

Summary

The Pictish and earlier neolithic history of Strathearn has been sadly neglected perhaps due to a certain aura of mystery and uncertainty which has shielded it from the prying eyes of 19th and early 20 th century historians. Reference to "Druids" and "Druidic circles" in the Statistical Accounts clearly illustrates the inbred antagonism held by the clerics of the period against anything smacking of paganism or mysticism. The early people were clearly skilled farmers and the artistic skills of their sculptors and metal workers have more recently been incorporated into contemporary designs by the craftsmen of the 21st century. The book *The Problem of the Picts* published in 1955 was as an attempt by a group of eminent historians including Professor Wainwright of Dundee, Professor Stuart Piggot and Professor K H Jackson to examine the mysteries surrounding the Picts Since then there have been a plethora of publications and research which has helped to put in perspective the role of these enigmatic peoples who are so much a part of our past. The recently opened Pictavia visitor centre at Brechin is not only a good day out but also a superb insight to our past displaying a veritable treasure chest of historical gems. The significance of Strathearn and its ancient Kingdom of Fortren should not be overlooked in the over picture of Scottish history.

Chapter 2

THE ARRIVAL OF THE ROMANS

Ardoch Camp (Above Braco, OS ref. NO 839 099)

One of the most important surviving Roman monuments in Britain. It was built at various times between the 80s and the 200s AD. Julius Agricola a Roman senator born in Gaul (France) was sent to govern Britain. He defeated the Caledonians at Mons Graupius. To secure their hold a succession of camps were built at Ardoch on the road north and some 30 miles north of Antonine's Wall. It was abandoned soon after 90 AD but reoccupied on their return 50 years later. It was modified once about 158 AD and finally abandoned about 163 AD after only 20 years.

It comprises a fort with camps and annexe. The Severan Camp extended to some 130 acres. The estimated strength of the Roman army at Mons Graupius was between 20,000 and 28,000. The Ardoch Camp had Spanish soldiers as well as Romans and housed around 5,000 troops. The Romans built a road running from Ardoch in a northeast direction to Kaims Castle where there was a fortlet. They must have been apprehensive about the locals because in the 6 miles from Ardoch to Strageath on the banks of the Earn there were 4 watchtowers plus the Kaims fortlet. The distance between each was about 1 000 yards.

Strageath was located on a plateau on the right bank of the Earn (OS ref. NN 894 180) and has been partially obliterated by the plough. Aerial photography shows it to have been about 3.5 acres and it housed two auxiliary regiments. Opinion is that the troops stationed here patrolled the road south to Ardoch and manned the watch towers (The Romans in Scotland, Gordon S Maxwell, 1989).

The Gask Ridge: On the north side of the Earn the Romans continued their defensive chain. Eleven watchtowers were constructed along the length of the Roman road to the Tay crossing at Bertha (it lies on the left bank of the Almond at its confluence with the Tay at what is now Inveralmond, north of Perth on the A9). These watch towers were larger than their counterparts between Ardoch and Strageath. Situated on the crest of the ridge they were well placed to carry out surveillance and communicate (probably by semaphore) with the next tower. Current studies of excavations on the Ridge are covered in the Internet web site The Roman Gask Project under the auspices of Dr David Woolliscroft and Dr Birgitta Hoffman of the Universities of Manchester and Liverpool. Nine excavations have been carried out to date (1998). It is now believed that the Gask frontier is the earliest Roman frontier in Britain built in the 80s AD 40 years before Hadrian's Wall and 60 years before the Antonine Wall. Since German archaeologists have now redated the start of their frontier (which was once thought to belong to the 80s) to the period known as the Trajanic, some 15 to 20 years later, it now seems that the Gask system is the first Roman frontier anywhere.

The sites on the ridge are as follows:

1. **Parkneuk** (NN 916 185): a signal station.

2. **Raith** (NN 932 186): a signal station.

3. **Ardunie** (NN 946 188): a signal station.

4. **Roundlaw** (NN 958 189): a signal station.

5. **Kirkhill** (NN 967 188): a signal station.

6. **Muir O' Fauld** (NN 982 189): a signal station.

7. **Gask House** (NN 991 192): a signal station and just to the south of it a camp.

8. **Witch Knowe** (NN 997 197): a signal station.

9. **Moss Side** (NO 008 199): a signal station.

10. **Thorny Hill** (NO 020 205): a signal station.

11. **Westmuir** (NO 026 211): a signal station.

The line of the Roman road follows more or less the line of the signal towers and is shown on the Ordnance Survey Sheet 58.

Although in geographic terms the Gask Ridge is the high ground between Crieff and Perth between the towers numbers 1 to 11 listed above, historically it is a generic term applied to the Flavian line of forts and watch towers extending from Glenbank south of Ardoch (NN 812 058) and to the north of the Balhaldie "Little Chef" on the A9 to Bertha off the A9 near Inveralmond Industrial Estate, Perth (NO 097 267) on the north bank of the Almond at its confluence with the Tay. According to Dr Woolliscroft the number of known towers is now 18 (1999). It would appear that these were intervisible and that Romans communicated effectively by means of a kind of semaphore.

Dalginross

To the south of Comrie village (OS ref. NN 773 214) lies a Roman camp. Referred to as a "glenblocker" fort and part of the line of forts running from Drumquhassle to Strathcathro and including the famous Inchtuthill south of Spittalfield. In the mid 1970s the Cumbernauld Historical Society carried out a "field walking" exercise of a number of Roman sites in Strathearn including Dalginross. It had been regarded as up until than as being poorly dated. Erosion has destroyed the north eastern corner but excavation in 1963 indicated that the outer portion of the larger enclosure had probably not undergone permanent occupation. The camp had a granary and faced west wards. It controlled the upper Earn. Woolliscroft's Report tells that after this excavation when no finds whatever were recovered, the general assumption was that it was indeed Flavian in origin. However, after the Cumbernauld exercise things began to change. Artefacts of both Flavian and Antonine origin were found. The Antonine finds which were of a later period indicate that the Romans had not just abandoned and forgotten Dalginross in their withdrawal of the late 80s AD but as was the case with Ardoch and Strathgeath had been reoccupied, probably as a northern outpost after the Antonine Wall had been built some 60 years later.

Fendoch Fort (OS ref. NN 908 286)

Another "glen blocker", situated at the narrows of Glen Almond beyond the Foulford Inn at the southern end of the Sma' Glen it guards as it were, the side door to Strathtay. It was excavated in 1938, the buildings of the interior were timber and nothing can be seen above ground. The barracks housed 10 centuries of the military cohort (1 000 men). It had a double granary, separate officer's quarters and a courtyard. On the lower slopes of the rising ground to the south there are intermittent traces of an artificial terrace, all that remains of the aqueduct by which fresh water was led into the heart of the fort. Some 1100 yards to the north west of the fort on high ground was a timber watch tower. The importance about the excavations at Fendoch were that at the end of occupation the buildings had been carefully dismantled with the wooden framing being dug out of the founds. In other words it was a systematic withdrawal, not one of pressure from the awaiting hordes of Caledonians.

Past writings about the Romans in Strathearn

There have been great strides in excavation, aerial photography and other methods which reveal much of our past. If we look at writings of the last century and indeed the early 20th century, it is evident how much has changed. Porteous (*The History of Crieff, 1912*) comments "The Roman remains in Strathearn and the surrounding districts are none too numerous and may be mentioned here". He goes on to repeat the tale of the Ardoch

This pre First World War post card shows clearly the Roman site near Fendoch. The landscape here has changed dramatically with forestry development.

excavations at Braco. Apparently there used to be a subterranean passage from the Camp to Grinnan Hill. Tradition stated that this contained a large quantity of hidden valuables:

> *"Between the camp at Ardoch and the Grinnan Hill o' Keir*
>
> *Lie seven kings ransoms for seven hundred year"*

This apparently was in the 17th century and the legend states that a criminal was offered his life by the Regality Court if he would agree to be lowered into the abyss and have a look. When he was drawn up he brought some Roman armour with him but in his second descent was suffocated. The armour was preserved in Ardoch House but in 1751 "was carried off by the Highlanders and its whereabouts is now unknown".

"In 1720 the entrance to the passage was covered with a large stone. A monument of Ammonius Damion now preserved in Glasgow University was discovered here and is remarkable as bearing the only Roman inscription found in the Roman province north of the Forth." Porteous means the Hunterian Museum in Glasgow. Unfortunately a recent (1998) visit there revealed it not to be on display and is "somewhere in our storage as we have so many things to show". Like the "kind gallows of Crieff" now in Perth Museum, there are undoubtedly sound arguments for the restoration of such artefacts to their original home.

There has been reported that during the construction of Burrell Street and King Street, evidence of a Roman road was discovered.

Another oft told tale is that of Lix Toll at the end of Glen Dochart at the Killin road end. It has been said that Lix is from the Roman numbers Ll X or 49 the 49th Legion. Whether such a tale is true is unsubstantiated.

Conclusions

The last decade of the old century saw a vast of amount of research into the Roman presence in Strathearn. Much of the credit goes to Drs D J Woolliscroft and Birgitta Hoffmann of Manchester and Liverpool Universities who have documented so much that is new about the Roman sojourn in the Strath. Their active digs in the summer months continue to extend our knowledge. Finds such as the Roman temporary camp at East Mid Lamberkin west of Perth. Although identified some 40 years prior to the excavations, it was only now that its actual significance can be confirmed. Such ongoing finds confirm how important Strathearn was in Roman Scotland.

Chapter 3

THE EARLS OF STRATHEARN

After the Battle of Lumphanan in 1057 when Malcolm Canmore defeated Macbeth, the emergent nation of Scotland was predominantly Irish / Celtic. It had a tribal structure with mormaers or toiseachs ruling the major provinces as autonomous Princes under the high King, father of the people. The former province or Kingdom of Fortren became the Earldom or Mormaership of Strathearn. This was essentially a Pictish structure. RA Dodgson (1981) traces a possible evolution from a Pictish division of Alba into two ie north and south of the Mounth. That established the Mormaerships or deputies to the "High King". Despite the change to the feudalism introduced by David 1 who had been brought up in Norman ways, Strathearn survived as a Celtic earldom after 1286. The Earldoms were sub divided into thanages such as Balquhidder in West Strathearn. These thanages had a thaneston where the thane lived and often a "kirkton". It is possible that the "pit" names of Pictish Strathearn may conceal the locations of the ancient tribal capitals.

According to Porteous, the name of Malise, Earl of Strathearn appears on a charter founding the monastery at Scone. He was succeeded by his son Ferteth or Ferquhard. He conspired with the other five Mormaers against Malcolm who had antagonised the people with his homage to the English King Henry II. There was near rebellion and eventually Malcolm sought peace with his Earls. Ferteth was succeeded by his son Gilbert who with the feudalising of the land was the first to receive charters from the King. Muthill (1172 /78) and Madderty in 1185 were the first. At this time there was a minor uprising against King William led by Gillecolm whose title was Marshal and is said to have occupied Dundurn.

The Earldom of Strathearn now stretched from Newburgh in the east to Balquhidder in the west. Inchaffrey Abbey was founded in 1200 and the name Crieff first appears in the charters. One witness is described as Bricius, the parson of Crieff (about 1199).

Earl Gilbert did well for himself. He married Matilda, daughter of the Earl of Arundel (to become the Norfolks). He had 8 sons and 3 daughters. He took a prominent part in the coronation of Alexander II in 1214. He died in 1223 and was succeeded by Robert a great supporter of Inchaffrey, having initially quarrelled with the Abbot over their possessions. He signed a charter in the 1222 in the ancient Church of Strageath The Earls of Strathearn were very important play makers in the King's business. Malise who succeeded Robert attended the coronation of Alexander lll in 1249. The king was only 8! The young King married Margaret daughter of King Henry of England 2 years later. Henry tried to inveigle his way into Scottish affairs but the young King resisted. Malise was in the favour of the English King and was appointed co Regent (there were 15 in number) to govern Scotland until Alexander reached 21. Malise married 4 times and as a result inherited more land and property. From his first wife Marjory he obtained lands in Northumberland. From his second wife Matilda, daughter of the Earl of Caithness and Orkney he obtained the Barony of Cortachy in Angus. He then married Emma and lastly Maria, widow of Magnus, King of Man. The account of Malise tells how he used his rights to "sell" many of the poorer classes into service of the Church at Inchaffrey. He died in 1271.

His son also Malise (III) was made a Regent to the Maid of Norway, Margaret. Malise was in collusion with Edward I and was a party to the signing of the Treaty of Salisbury by which the Scottish Estates agreed to the marriage of Edward's son to the young maid and heiress to the Scottish throne. She died and history was changed.

It should be emphasised the Earls of Strathearn were amongst the leading nobility in Scotland. The Pope when addressing the See of Dunblane wrote directly to the Earl. He married the sister of John Comyn, Earl of Buchan. Malise was an Anglophile and in 1291 paid homage to Edward I at Stirling. He supported Balliol. He followed him when he invaded Cumberland and ravaged the country. In fact he was captured but soon released and paid further homage to Edward. His sons were residing at the English Court. In 1303 Malise was with the English army at Perth dining with the Prince of Wales. As Bruce gained the favour and support of the Scottish nobility and was crowned king at Scone in 1306, Malise continued his support for Edward. Bruce delivered an ultimatum to him via the Abbot of Inchaffrey, to acknowledge his sovereignty but the reply was curt: *"Nay, I have nothing to do with him"*.

Bruce and the Earl of Atholl marched into Strathearn to Fowlis, at that time the chief castle of the Earldom. Malise had now retired to the wood of Crieff (Callum's Hill?) with his retainers. Bruce delivered another ultimatum. Malise met with him but refused to swear fealty and departed under a safe conduct arrangement. Malise blew it when he met with the Earl of Atholl and insulted him over his loyalty to Bruce. The incensed Atholl persuaded Bruce to withdraw safe conduct from Malise who was taken prisoner and sent to Inchcolm on the Firth of Forth. His obstinacy continued until death was threatened and he duly performed homage to Bruce. This was never true and when asked to march with Bruce against the Earl of Pembroke, refused. He was besieged at Castle Cluggie (Ochtertyre). Malise spoke with

Bruce but nothing transpired to change matters. Thereafter Bruce was defeated at Methven by the Earl of Pembroke. Malise was a born loser. He was captured by his English friends and charged with treason for swearing fealty to Bruce whilst on Inchcolm. He was confined to Rochester Castle *"but not in chains"* by Edward. His son also Malise was detained at Carlisle. Malise was tried at Westminster, but acquitted having stated that his loyalty to Bruce was forced upon him under threat of death. thereafter he remained loyal to the English. His son however threw in his lot with Bruce and when Perth was stormed son captured father. He died shortly thereafter and was buried in Inchaffrey Abbey to the right of the high alter.

The future of The Celtic Earls of Strathearn was heading towards a certain end. Their duplicity and opposition to Bruce were their ultimate downfall. Of Malise IV the tale of Tom a Chastile is told elsewhere. He seemed to have regained at one time some of the lost importance thrown away by his father, as he is the fourth signatory to the Declaration of Arbroath. What happened to him is uncertain. Malise V paid the penalty of his forefathers. Baliol had granted the title to the Earl of Surrey and it was claimed that Malise III had stood down voluntarily. In 1344 David ll would not reinstate him and granted the title to Maurice Moray.

Moray's tenure was short lived. He was killed at the Battle of Durham and the title remained dormant for a number of years. In 1370 Robert II conferred the title upon his son David.

The title passed to the Graham family when David's daughter married Patrick Graham. The animosity between the Drummonds and Murrays arose from a court case where Sir Alexander Murray, a brother in law of the King, declined to appear before Sir John Drummond, Steward of Strathearn on a murder charge. Eventually he did with much bad feeling.

In 1413, Sir Patrick Graham, Earl of Strathearn was forced by the Murray family to remove Sir John Drummond from office. In the park at Ferntower Sir John killed Earl Patrick and took flight to Ireland and was never heard of again. Malise Graham became Earl on the death of his mother in 1408. He was delivered as a hostage for the release of James l from England. James coveted the title and claimed that the Graham claim was faulty. He thus annexed it to the Crown and ended the long line of independent Earls of Strathearn.

Chapter 4

THE WEAVERS OF STRATHEARN

Some two hundred and fifty years ago, the unpaved streets of Crieff resembled more El Paso than the douce Perthshire town of the present.Those were the days of the Tryst when drovers from as far away as Caithness in the north and Skye and Kintyre in the west brought their beasts to the "meeting place".

Things however were changing and between 1760 and 1770 there was a considerable decline in trade. The reasons for this were many but drovers were now heading to Falkirk or more specifically Larbert where grazing was cheaper and its location was more convenient for the traders from Central Scotland and indeed from England.

For Strathearn, the diminution in importance of the Michaelmas Fair or Market brought about by the collapse of the cattle trade, was to a certain extent offset by the rapid growth of the linen trade. Traditionally, rural communities had always had a weaving tradition although mostly in wool. With the Union of Parliaments, the protective tariffs set up by the English state were abolished and at last Scottish merchants were given equal opportunities to deal with the lucrative London market where the light, cheap linen cloths had begun to usurp the hold of the traditional woollen garment.

A "count" of heads in Scotland had been carried out around 1755 by Dr Webster. This is a useful base to compare with later figures. Indeed in The Statistical Account of Scotland edited by Sir John Sinclair and covering the period 1791 to 1799, the contributors for each parish, invariably the local minister, estimated the local population. Although this cannot be regarded as absolutely correct it does allow us to draw comparisons with the earlier statistics and come to some interesting conclusions.

TABLE ONE	POPULATION			
PARISH	*1755*	*1790's*	*1801*	*1835*
CRIEFF	1914	2640	2876	4306
COMRIE	2546	3000	2458	2622
MUTHILL	2902	2949	2880	3421
AUCHTERARDER	1194	1670	2042	3315

As can be seen, the principal centres of population all showed considerable increase in the later part of the 18th century. One of the reasons was clearly the rise in handloom weaving. Some of the contemporary and 19th century accounts portray vividly the position in the towns and villages of Strathearn.

Reid's *Annals of Auchterarder* quotes thus: "Handloom weaving, principally for the Indian trade, was 60 years ago,* the staple industry of the place. In the town and the neighbouring village of Aberuthven there would be upwards of 500 weavers."

Going back to the Statistical Account, the accounts given by the ministers are most revealing in their description of the weaving trade of the time. Although their job was that of saving souls they had a position of great importance within the community. Their bias against faiths other than the established church was very noticeable and the vitriolic comments on those of other persuasions perhaps reflected on the turbulent passage of time over the last century when the control of the "Church" was in some doubt. With regard to what actually was happening within their Parish, it is clear that in most cases they endeavoured to paint a picture that gave a true reflection on the every day life of their parishioners.

Comrie

Looking at the Parish of Comrie in the 1792/93 Account, we note that the staple industry is linen yarn "of which a great quantity is spun and sold each year. With the money which this yarn brings, most of the farmers pay a great part of their rents. This yarn sells at about 2/4 per spindle" (i.e. about 11 pence in present currency). Very much a cottage industry, the small farmers or cottars produced a variety of cloths to suit their needs. The lint was spun into a yarn and from that a cloth was produced. The finer cloth was made into men and women's shirts whilst the coarser was turned into "sailors jackets and trousers". Comrie in the 18th century was a Highland village unlike its near neighbour Crieff some seven miles to the east. The women of the Parish produced a great quantity of "plaiden cloth" and a considerable quantity of tartan from which they made plaids and hose. The Account tells us these products were partly for home use and partly for the market.

The second Account in 1844 relates that *"the manufacture of cotton and woollen cloth is carried on in the Parish. The hand loom cotton weavers are employed by houses in Glasgow and Perth. During the winter months, 136 hand loom weavers are employed and of these only one tenth are employed during the three months of winter. The remaining 120 may, on an average, earn 1/- (one shilling or five pence decimal) per day, for 280 days in the year, that is deducting 30 days in the harvest, and Sundays, and other occasional vacant days, sixty five. Of these there are about 50 heads of families who have each good gardens, and a patch of potatoes, and a pig,*

*This refers to the year 1837.

which may add about £ 4/10/0 (£4.50 decimal) to each family's income. The only woollen manufacture is carried on at the River Lednock, in the village of Comrie. Eleven men and eight children are employed at the mill, and five persons are employed out of doors."

Shortly after this picture of what was an apparently thriving industry things changed rapidly. The day of the cottage industry was over as more and more factories in the industrial belt sprang up undercutting prices and offering steady, regular employment. As with other parts of the Highlands emigration denuded the glens of their industrious occupants. Many Comrie people sailed for Canada.

Muthill

Moving across to the adjoining parish of Muthill, we find a similar pattern of life albeit that most of the area can be termed Lowland rather than Highland. The Muthill Parish Account is to all intents and purposes a more detailed report on the conditions in the parish than that given for Comrie. The Rev. John Scott tells us in some detail the population break down according to religious beliefs. You can sense his glee and air of superiority when we are informed that there are 2843 Protestants "of all persuasions and ages" and a mere 59 "Papists"! The good Reverend notes that since Webster's population survey some 40 years earlier, both in the rural part of the Parish as well as the village of Muthill, the population had risen. The Account attributes this to the increase in the number of farms by sub division into smaller units (strange in light of the converse happening elsewhere at that time) and in Muthill itself the increase is attributed to the increase feuing and building. There is little mention of weaving activity apart from a brief note that there were "4 flax mills, 3 of which have been erected lately" and that there is a "cotton work on a small scale".

In the 50 years that had elapsed since the first Account, the Parish had undergone substantial changes. The population had risen by some 16% and the author of the second report in 1844 gives the split down into three parts. Muthill village had some 1210 persons, Braco village some 384 persons and living and working in the country was a staggering 1827, involved in a labour intensive farming industry! The Rev. James Walker seems somewhat pre occupied by the ecclesiastical condition of his flock rather than elaborating on the industry or trades prevailing at the time. Indeed he comes over in a rather patronising and superior way when he describes his brethren thus: *"Of the inhabitants we may safely say, that they live comfortably and soberly, and at peace with one another. We have not the temptations of a populous city to contend with neither have we the influx of strangers to captivate us with their novelties and often times their vices. Neither have we any residenters wasting overgrown fortunes amongst us, and exciting the envy or dislike of their poorer fellow men. But we have a rural and simple hearted people, remarkably kind to each other, and given to rejoice, and weep with them that weep."*

Weaving was still an important part of the economy although it appears that Muthill was not so orientated in that direction as neighbouring Crieff, Comrie and Auchterarder. It is reported that the village had "about 60 of its inhabitants employed in weaving cotton which is sent to them from Glasgow."

Auchterarder

The "Lang Toon" of Auchterarder was very much into weaving as an important part of the town's economy. Our first real insight into this was the revelations contained in the First Statistical account written around 1775 by Reverend Andrew Duncan. He tells us that at that time the town had 49 weavers. There is criticism however of the methods employed by the weavers and their associates.

"About 20 years ago a considerable manufacture of yarn and narrow linen cloth was carried out in Auchterarder. It was fold bleached and unbleached, and exported to Glasgow. But this trade is now in a great measure extinct. Sale linens are still manufactured in the town and neighbourhood; and linen, of a fabric peculiar to the place, and which goes by its name."

Outside Auchterarder lay the "village" known as Borland Park which had been built by the Government "after the war in 1763". This referred to the end of the Seven Years War when Britain clashed with France in North America. Despite the fact that this "model" village reflected a "generous" settlement it was obviously a bit of a flop with most of the planted soldiers leaving shortly after its foundation. Despite this factor the good Reverend tells us that its 140 or so inhabitants were mostly weavers.

What we learn about the modus operandi of the weaving and its associated trades was, that according to Duncan, "Were the two handed spinning wheel more used, it would probably contribute in some measure to better the circumstances of the lower class of people as well as to increase the materials of the linen manufacture. There are but one or two such wheels in this Parish and it is but little used in many parts of the country. It might also be for the interests of the lower classes of people, and especially the women, were they more employed than they are, in manufactures for which they are qualified. The great demand for men for all kinds of work, has raised their wages to an exorbitant height, whilst in this part of the country, at least, the wages of female servants are barely sufficient to support them when in health."

On reflection one wonders at the somewhat chauvinistic attitude of the cleric towards both the female sex and the "lower classes" amongst his parishioners. Indeed such a knowledge with regard to the workings of the intricacies of the spinning wheel would no doubt have been a useful tool for them to prosper above their station!

The next Statistical Account was published some 54 years later in 1844. In that time much had changed not only in Strathearn but also in Scotland as a whole. The author of the Auchterarder contribution, Mr James Aitken, based his report on information gleaned in 1836/1837. It is dated "May 1837".

In the period between the two accounts the population had doubled from 1670 persons to 3315. Four times as many people were involved in manufacturing than in agriculture.

According to the author the trade of the town consisted mostly of weaving cotton supplied from Glasgow. There were upwards of 500 looms in the Parish whilst on the Water of Ruthven there were 13 mills or "manu-factories" on a small scale. These included two linseed oil mills, two flax mills, a fulling mill and a woollen manufactory of shawls and blankets and similar materials. These were indeed the boom times for both the cottage industry and the power looms of the new water powered factories.

The last of the "Accounts" was that published in 1953 and revised in 1962. This was just too early to record the final death throws of the local textile industry. After a thriving period, the changing pattern of world trade coupled with the cheap labour of the third world proved just too much.

"The chief trade of Auchterarder is, as it has been for well over a century, textiles. Over 100 years ago, Auchterarder and Aberuthven were chiefly occupied by hand loom weavers. These depended on middle men who supplied the yarn to the weavers and bought the finished cloth to sell in Glasgow. William Hally was one such. In 1850 he established a business in Borland Park. In 1863 he opened the Castleton Mill and in 1869 the firm of Hally and Co., which emerged from this, introduced 60 power looms In 1872 the first of their Ruthvenvale Mills was built with 25 power looms; in 1874 the same firm had the Dollerie Mill in Crieff; in 1880 all 3 mills were incorporated at Ruthvenvale. In 1883 in this mill there were 453 looms with 300 workers. In 1892 the mill was extended with 540 looms and between 300 and 400 workers. Cloth was exported to Australia, India, China and New Zealand, but not to Europe, while there was also a vigorous home trade. Seventy per cent of the raw material was imported from Belgium and 70 per cent of the finished article exported. In the inter war years, there was here, as in other mills throughout the country, a great slump in trade. Despite modernisation carried out after the war, all weaving ceased in this mill at the end of 1956. In 1929 a knitwear business started and is now the only activity on the premises with 20 employees. This firm goes by the name of Gleneagles Knitwear Co., 80% of its products being exported to America. Only 5,000 square feet of the premises out of a total 65,000 square feet are being used. The firm of Robert White and Co. has experienced similar development. This business began in the 1840s with hand looms in individual houses. The first factory was situated off the High Street in what is now known as Kinnoul Place. It comprises two rows of buildings, one containing dwelling houses with hand looms, the other housing hand looms only. The present building, Glenruthven Mills was built about 1874. It houses 60 single width looms, which make shirtings and material for blouses and

ties. In 1959, 6 double width looms capable of making light weight worsteds were added. The normal number of employees is about 40, 16 men and 24 women."

And so endeth a period in the history of the Town which looked at one time as if there would be an orderly transition from the early hand loom weavers to the power loom factories and eventually into full scale manufacture. It was not to be. Like so many industries in this country it succumbed to unforeseen economic pressures both from home and abroad. A proud tradition had died out and is now all but forgotten.

Dunning

The Parish of Dunning is as ancient as any of its Strathearn neighbours. Unlike some of them it retains a deep feeling for its past and its Local History Society has proven itself innovative and forward thinking. Indeed its web page attracts "hits" from all over and its presentation of local history through the internet surely is the sign post to the future. According to Dr Webster the Parish had a population of 1491 in 1775 which by the time of the First Statistical Account had grown to about 1600. Steady increase over the next few decades saw it rise to some 2125 in 1841. As can be seen, comparison with the other parishes shows Dunning lagging substantially behind adjoining Auchterader in terms of growth (43% compared with 178%) and Crieff (43% to 125%), but well ahead of both Muthill and Comrie. Here we see signs of the growing urbanisation that effected Scotland as the drift from the country side accelerated with the rapid growth of industry and mechanisation.

In the First Statistical Account on the Parish written somewhat anonymously by "a Friend to Statistical Inquiries" (it was the norm for the Parish minister to carry out this task), there is an interesting section dealing with the tradesmen of the period in Dunning.

"The only manufacture carried on here is the making of a few course linens for the Glasgow and Perth markets. Weavers in the Parish, 63, about 40 of whom are employed in factory work". It goes on later to state that *"the blue bonnet is not altogether out of fashion in this part of the country – a considerable quantity of coarse linen is spun by the women in the Parish, not a few of whom spin on the two-handed wheel, which a good many years ago was introduced from Fife."*

In the Second Account written by the Rev Dr Russell in 1842, little concerning the weaving trade attracts the good doctor's attention. In a brief passing comment he points out that *"A greater proportion of the inhabitants are weavers, and are supplied with work from Glasgow."*

Redgorton

It is perhaps stretching it somewhat to deviate from the geographic boundaries of the Strath, but so important is the neighbouring Parish of Redgorton that its inclusion helps emphasise that outwith the modest mills at Auchterarder and Crieff there were in this adjoining place a significant mechanised spinning industry which rivalled in many ways, the famed New Lanark mills of Dale and Owen.

The village of Stanley so called after the family name of the Earls of Derby who were related by marriage to Dukes of Atholl, was planned around the spinning mill on the banks of the Tay designed by Richard Arkwright. Recently renovated to provide homes for Perth's burgeoning population, it stands as a remarkable monument to a by gone age. Like New Lanark it developed cotton commercially, spinning the thread that was turned into the cloth that the country's expanding population required. Sadly cotton was caught in the in the politics of the time. The Napoleonic wars and the subsequent downturn in trade saw the mill close in 1812 for nine years. When it reopened, demand soared and soon it was employing some 2,000 operatives. The American Civil War saw the supply of the raw material dry up and once again the mill closed.

Thereafter things never quite got back to normal and after a short spell producing acrylic fibres in the 1980s the mill finally closed for ever in 1989.

Crieff

The town of Crieff too, had developed its own weaving "industry" in the wake of the decline after the departure of the Tryst to Falkirk. It was prior to the '45 Rising when James Drummond, Third Duke of Perth opened a linen "factory" on the site of what is now the District Library at the junction of Lodge Brae and Comrie Street. Known as the Mason's Hall part of it is still owned by the Masonic Lodge and one can see the much worn stone embellishment on the front facade with the inscription "St Michael's Lodge" still visible.

No doubt Drummond's Jacobite sympathies were the root cause of the factory's destruction by the Hanoverian troops in 1746 but so ended the initial attempt to establish a viable textile trade within the town. In reflection this would have undoubtedly have assisted the local economy of the time. With the Tryst still active for about another 20 or so years, the down turn in local trade may have been averted.

Irrespective of ones attitude to the parties of conflict, it is clear that out of chaos came a semblance of normality and hope. The Government appointed Commissioners to administer the confiscated estates of the deposed Jacobites including the Perth family, until then the dominant Strathearn lairds. A concerted effort was made to establish the linen trade in Crieff. Ground was made available to feu out (ie to lease in perpetuity) to enable the individual to build a home with a small garden in which he could grow flax to be spun into linen. The Commissioners also assisted in the development of the linen industry by providing water power for scutching mills at nominal rentals or feus. Scutching was the process which treated the flax prior to heckling and the final spinning of the thread. When the dried flax stalks were going through the scutching mill, the "scutchers" threw off a great deal off refuse which was known as pob or pob-tow and was used by the poorer people as fuel. According to Porteous the chief burners of pob-tow were the inhabitants of Bridgend.

There were several scutching mills in operation and they worked mainly in the winter months. Because of the dust, it became obligatory for the thirsty deliverers of flax to receive a bottle of whisky per load! The spinning of the flax was normally the work of the women folk. Prior to it being spun it was heckled or broken down. The Meadows or Town Green was the principal area of the Crieff where the webs of linen were laid out for bleaching.

It was John Drummond, Second Earl of Perth who had brought the first Flemish weavers to Strathearn in the early part of the 17th century. Prior to linen, wool was spun and woven. Waulk and fulling mills were established near Turret Bridge in what is now Mungall Park and at Drummond Castle in the earlier part of the 18th Century. These prepared and shrank the cloth. Towards the end of the 18th Century a small company carried on a woollen "manufactory" at Dallerie. Another such "manufactory" was established at the south side of James Square where the Golf Shop is now located (1998). The building was known as the Warehouse or locally as Mount Rascal. James McEwan established the Dallerie Woollen Mills which specialised in tartan cloth. It was later bought by Hally and Co of Auchterarder. The Earnvale Woollen Mill was established by James Mitchell at the end of the laid opposite Braidhaugh and functioned for a number of years. It had a somewhat chequered career having been damaged by fire on more than one occasion. The buildings can still be seen from the bridge although they now serve as workshops for Derek Halley, landscape contractor (1999). With planning permission having been granted for a housing development yet another piece of Crieff's diminishing industrial heritage is scheduled to disappear before very long.

Commercially wool became an important part of the town's economy. As with Auchterarder, it developed eventually along power loom lines and utilised the water power of the nearby River Earn and the Turret Burn. An examination of the 1901 ordnance survey map of the area clearly shows the utilisation of this resource with the construction of a lade from the weir at what is the top end of MacRosty Park southwards till it joined the Earn opposite the Braidhaugh at the bridge. The lade with its multiplicity of sluices is sadly no more. The storms of the '80s brought torrential rainfall to the upper reaches of the Turret and the violent flood waters caused havoc lower down with the result that the weir was severely damaged and the lade left high and dry. Despite plans and proposals it appears unlikely that water will flow again down its course. In its hay day, there was a saw mill and a corn mill at Milnab on the site of what is now Park Manor (see page 119). Further down at the entrance to Morrison' s playing fields at Dallerie was a large and for a long time, a prosperous woollen mill. Established at the end of the 18th century and run by one John McQueen it did not really come to prominence until it was taken over by James McEwan who had been as noted above, been in business on the east side of James Square with a William Hamilton. The business of James McEwan and Sons became famous for its tartans and for the early part of the 18th century employed a large number of people as power loom weavers. The business and premises at Dallerie were purchased in the 1870s by Hallys of Auchterarder who invested money in new buildings and equipment and for a while employed upwards of 300 persons. In a process of rationalisation the works were closed after a little over 10 years and business transferred to their Ruthvenvale Mill in the "Lang Toon". The factory then became a dyeing and cleaning establishment and eventually was bought and run by the Crieff Hydro as the Strathearn Steam Laundry Company.

A prosperous community?

It can be seen from the above that the weavers were virtually a community within a community. They often lived in specific locations within a town or village and from the late 18th century developed an individuality that was strongly apparent. In *Parish Life in Eighteenth Century Scotland* (Steven M, 1995) the author highlights the Statistical Account of Caputh, north of Perth where the minister highlighted conveniently the annual budget of a weaving family comprising the weaver, his wife and three small bairns under five years of age. As Caputh is on the edge of Strathearn, the use of these figures is considered apposite to their contemporaries in the Strath. The weekly income was assessed at 9/- or 45 pence and the expenditure 5/11 or approximately 30 pence. This outgoing was listed as three pecks of oat meal, two pecks of barley, milk, salt, onions, potatoes, butter, cheese, bacon and meat, soap, starch, blue and oil, thread, thrum and worsted. Out of the weekly surplus of 3/1 or 16 pence had to met certain annual costs which were listed as a man's suit, jacket and breeches, hat and handkerchief, 2 shirts, a pair of stockings and for his wife a gown and petticoat, 2 shifts a pair of shoes, two aprons a pair of stockings handkerchief, and caps, children's clothes, fuel and most importantly, money to cover such contingencies as *"lying in, sickness, loss of time thereby and burials, one year with another"*. This came to a total of some five pounds thirteen shillings and six pence leaving an annual surplus in the family budget of over two pounds or 30% of gross income! The missing factor from this equation is carefully added to the Account, *"the cost of housing being a rent of one pound for both house and garden."* The family's food is from *"the garden, dressed by the man in the mornings and evenings, and affords them cabbages, greens and potatoes, to the amount of the rent."*

The Status and Politics of the Weaver

Unlike many of the rural areas of Scotland, the weavers in industrial centres such as Glasgow and Paisley were politically active being involved both in protests about cheap labour and imports as well as with electoral reform. The influx of Irish labour posed a threat to their status. The trade was comparatively easy to learn and the cosy paternalism of many of the factories where spinners and hand loom weavers and their families had worked for many years came under threat. The weavers organised and protested against change including special taxes levied against them but were usually defeated in their attempts as the acts of protest were called riots and dispersed forcibly by troops. In Strathearn as else where the return of soldiers after the Napoleonic Wars in 1815 and the situation of no work and high prices seriously alarmed the government. Weavers became involved in movements for reform and in Glasgow the Calton riots saw 47 weavers arrested and put on trial for treason. Three were convicted and executed. James Wilson was hanged and beheaded (the special procedure for treason) on Glasgow Green on the 30th August 1820, whilst the other two John Baird and Andrew Hardie were tried in Stirling and hanged and beheaded on the 8th of September of the same year.

In Strathearn things were not quite as politically explosive as in the industrial west of Scotland. The passions of reform had however reached here as well. The following account of the action played by the Crieff weavers is graphically recalled in *Crieff Traditions and Characters* (Macara, 1881).

"A special meeting was held on 6th May 1831 when it was resolved that an address be transmitted to His Majesty William IV for what he has done in supporting his ministers in reforming the representation of his subjects and dissolution of Parliament. It was also resolved to assemble in the Market Park on 12th May and to send orders to the Comrie and Muthill weavers to put in an appearance. The day came round and the utmost excitement prevailed amongst the congregated thousands." The minute detailing the affair is dated *"Town Park Crieff, 12th May 1831"* and says *"This Society along with the rest of the societies having assembled and after an able address by Mr John Kidd, Preses of the Shoemaker's Society, to His Majesty King William IV the procession moved on three and three through the principal streets of the town, South Bridgend etc returned to the Town Park and dismissed with the greatest of regularity. They then assembled in the Mason's Hall and the Weaver's Hall when appropriate sentiments were given and the health of these brave men who supported the Reformers were given and drunk with great applause. The scene of the day closed with a fine display of fireworks and passed with the greatest of harmony. Addresses were also delivered by Dr Fyfe, William Clement, merchant, John McNab, weaver and John M'Farlane, shoemaker. This procession was in reality a general procession of the inhabitants of the district. Each trade society and party had appropriate banners and equipments and each had its band of music. The procession was about half a mile in length and the day was a red letter one for all who witnessed these doings, and old people still look back to it*

with admiration through the vista of half a century."

The Weavers Society of Crieff

Weaving and spinning had grown over the years from being merely an adjunct to normal agricultural operations to a thriving cottage industry by the 18th century. In most cases it was the farmer's wife who would have spun the wool from the sheep and follow this through by weaving a rough cloth to be turned into garments for her family. Sometimes the spun wool would be sold to the village weaver who in his loom shed would convert the raw material into usable cloth. The invention of the hand loom by Joseph Loom in Flanders in the early 1700s had revolutionised things dramatically.

The number of weavers and associated trades had grown rapidly in the villages of Strathearn. In 1768 the Weavers Society was formed in Crieff. Each weaver paid into a fund to support the families of those of his trade to ensure that their widows and their orphans would not be left destitute. A code of rules and regulations were drawn up by the eight founding members and approved in 1770. Such was the success of the new Society that year by the year numbers grew.

At a meeting held on the 9th November 1775, it was resolved to have an annual procession and to purchase the necessary flags etc., for such occasions. Again the only extant account seems to be that published by Macara in 1881.

"Immediately after this meeting they set about getting the colours with all possible speed and employed a painter in Paisley to paint after the pattern of their colours at Paisley and they were soon got home and their price was for six yards of crimson silk £2. 2s; for painting £2. 2s; for the pole to carry them 1/6; for the iron and brass for the top of the pole 2/-; for two tassels 5/-. There was also got 12 1/2 yards of crimson Persian silk for sashes at two shillings and four pence per yard. There was also provided 80 rods to carry in their hands at 1/2d each. Having got every thing provided necessary for the procession they agreed to have their parade on the 4th day of June 1776 years, being His Majesty's birthday, George III, and a good number of the brethren being present they having by this time increased to about 80 and so after choosing persons to bear office for the ensuing year and going through some other business, they for the first time made a very regular and orderly procession through the town between five and six o'clock in the afternoon, having a very good band of music attending them, and after the parade spent the night in taking a glass with one another in a most cheerful and harmonious manner.

What would the present natives not give to have a photograph and detailed account of this procession? The appearance of the actors, their dresses, demeanour, size, style have marching, and the music and musical instruments to which they marched? Also the appearance of the streets, made of rows of thatched biggings, and the crowds of onlookers would make a most interesting and instructive study. The annual processions thereafter were sights worth seeing, and the rural inhabitants crowded the village on such occasions. On the 4th of June 1795 " a petition from the brethren in Comrie was presented craving that the Society would grant them the favour of the colours and the sashes belonging the corporation upon the 13th day of July next, in order that they might have a parade on that day, which they think might be for the honour and advantage of the Society, and that a number of the members from Crieff might attend, "which petition was unanimously agreed unto. At a meeting held on 19th June 1781, the members of the Society belonging to Auchterarder craved authority to be allowed to erect themselves into a Society at Auchterarder, and they would pay instantly five shillings as an acknowledgement of having sprung from the Crieff Society; which was agreed to". A similar petition came from Fowlis Wester in 1819, and Muthill followed suit in 1822, and they solicit us (not only as being their maternal society, but being the first and most honourable society in Scotland) for obtaining the weaver craft."

The site of the Hall was in Commissioner Street or to be specific Scott Terrace and was rebuilt and turned into flats around the 1930s.

The demise of the weavers in Crieff

The demography below shows the sad eclipse of the weavers as a close knit group! They were aging and unemployed. The CEBs (census enumeration books) which provide such a rich source of identifying patterns fail somewhat in the instance of the weavers as a trade. Indeed from the first census of 1841 through 1851, 61, 71, 81 and finally 1891 they fail to differentiate fully between power loom (plw) and hand loom (hlw) weavers which was the intention of the Registrar General for Scotland as noted in the notes to the enumeration books. This has reduced considerably the efficacy of relevant analysis. Murray's book *The Scottish Hand Loom Weavers 1790-1850* (Murray N, 1978) provides one of the few detailed accounts of the part the weavers played in the overall story of this country. We can by comparing his overall figures with those abstracted from the Crieff CEBs gain some indication as to how Crieff compared with the overall Scottish situation (Fig 1).

FIGURE 1

Crieff				Scotland		
Year	*Weavers*	*Population*	*%*	*Weavers*	*Population*	*%*
1841	650	4085	16	84560	2620184	3
1851	436	4504	10	25000	2888742	1
1861	120	4300	3	10000	3062294	>1
1871	121	4153	3	10000	3360018	>1
1881	28	4700	>1	4000	3735573	>1
1891	10	4902	>1	N/A	4025647	–

Figure 2 below is taken from the Census enumeration books for 1881 in Crieff and indicates that at a time when hand loom weaving in Scotland was very much on its uppers, the trade still in the Town was still alive, albeit that the participants were perhaps well past the first flush of youth.

FIGURE 2

An analysis of the Crieff weavers found in the 1881 Census

Names and location in Crieff

Miller Street
18   James McAra, wool weaver, 56yrs born Crieff

Mitchell Street
3   James Cramb, weaver, 72yrs born Crieff

Water Wynd (NB At the foot of what is now Mitchell Street)
William Hepburn, woollen weaver, 56yrs born Crieff

George Street **NB Now Strathearn Terrace
15   Duncan Kay, handloom weaver, 69yrs born Dull *speaks Gaelic

King Street
4   Alexander Smeaton, woolllen weaver, 68yrs born Crieff
5
43   Alex. McLaren, weaver, 68yrs born Crieff
44
99   William Miller, woollen weaver, 79yrs born Muthill
100
101   Alexander Cramb, cotton weaver, 40yrs born Crieff
*unemployed

Commissioner Street
35   Duncan Stalker, cotton weaver, 82yrs born Comrie *retired
Alexander McNab, weaver, 81yrs born Crieff
58 west Peter Hamilton, cotton weaver, 75yrs born Crieff *unemployed
Jane Haggart, woollen warper, 40yrs born Crieff *unemployed
20 east Jessie Cumming, powerloom wool weaver, 17yrs born Crieff
26   Catherine McLean, powerloom wool weaver, 24yrs born Crieff
Lodging house   William Fleming, tweed weaver, 63yrs born Leslie, Fife

Gallowhaugh
6   Thomas Morrison, formerly wool weaver, 69yrs born Crieff

North Bridge Street
4   Ann Roy, powerloom weaver, 36yrs born Crieff

| 43 | Peter McNeill Sn., wool warper, 84yrs born Muthill |
| 29 | Robert Morrison, woollen weaver, 58yrs born Crieff |

Comrie Street

Janet McNaughton, shirting weaver, 17yrs born Crieff

Upper Dallerie

Donald McAlpine, woollen manufacturer, 54yrs born Killin
*speaks Gaelic and employs 6 men and a boy

Burrell Street

| 70 | James Gowans, formerly woollen weaver, 76yrs born Crieff |
| 60 | William Sinclair, woollen weaver, 64yrs born Muthill |

Cemetery Road

3 (Yester Cottage) William Adamson, wool spinner, 64yrs born Alloa
    * lodger

Earnbank Road

David Allan, retired weaver, 88yrs born Crieff
John McOwan, woollen weaver, 67yrs born Crieff
Margaret McOwan, woollen winder, 67yrs born Monzievaird
Henry McOwan, woollen weaver, 32yrs born Crieff

As noted above the exact description given and recorded in the census returns is not always definitive enough to pin point the exact nature of the persons job but the table (Fig. 1) is indicative enough to illustrate that in Crieff and probably Strathearn as a whole the position of weaving and kindred trades was extremely important and was for a time the dominant occupation in the town's economy. If one looks at 1851 it can be seen that some 16% of the total population were engaged in weaving and kindred trades. Taking into account young children, the elderly and woman who did not work, the weavers as a percentage of the working population would at that time have reached around 30%, a not inconsiderable figure. By 1881 the position had rapidly altered. Looking at the few weavers remaining (Fig. 2) of the 28 identified their average age was close on sixty. Nineteen had been born in Crieff, three in nearby Muthill, one in Comrie and one in adjacent Monzievaird. Two came from what is known as Highland Perthshire (Killin and Dull) whilst the other two came from Fife and Alloa respectively.

The gender breakdown showed that 22 were men and only 6 women. What were living and working conditions like amongst the weavers? A letter written to the *Crieff Herald* in 1857 described conditions prevailing some 25 years earlier in 1832.

"It was a well known fact that before the railway commenced operations almost all the money which upheld our village was derived from agriculture and weaving; and

whatever other occupations were carried on within the village were dependent on these two for employment, and their work paid with the money paid from either of them. I do not wish to be misunderstood when I say that agriculture and the weaving trade solely upheld the village of Crieff 25 years ago; other minor sources might have helped and do so still; but I think that no one acquainted with our village will doubt, that if the money derived from the two above-mentioned sources now spent in Crieff were diverted into another channel, many of the shops would soon be found with closed doors. Such being facts, I shall take the liberty in the present letter of bringing to your notice the condition of those who earned their bread at the loom in Crieff 25 years ago. At the time the weaving was liable to fluctuations, the same as it is now, and so were provisions, but in not in such a ratio as in late years, and seldom of long duration.

But deductions on the price of work were small and of rare occurrence, and were undeserved, legal redress could easily be obtained. At that time also many working men had small plots of ground at an easy rent by the cultivation of which a great part of their winter's provision was provided. Many kept a pig, and got ground for the manure that they had collected thereby from any farmer in the neighbourhood for a crop of potatoes, so that when the pig was killed and the potatoes gathered in, the principal part of their winter's food was beside them, and if they were obliged to be idle a short time in winter they were not in such difficulties as wont of work creates at present. At that time there was hardly any failure of the potato crop and I have known a weaver have as many as ten bolls of potatoes grown from manure collected by himself and family, and which cost him no expense but tolls and no trouble but the cleaning and taking them out of the ground. At that time the neighbouring proprietors and farmers were not so careful of their withered or useless branches of trees or decayed herbage as they are now; neither had the fishing association of Perth arrived at the legal acme of perfection regarding the finny tribe which they now possess. For when the first of February had arrived they took no more concern with the River Earn until the net fishing ended on the 14th of September. Ever since that date of my recollections of the village of Crieff, namely 25 years ago, the cords have been tightening around the majority of the working population, so that between house rents, high priced provisions, high priced coals and other fuel (more so than in other places not many miles distant) deductions from the price of labour of the most unusual kinds, and a scarcity of work which has been of regular occurrence every winter except one for these last seven years, there is now a great change in the condition of those who earn their bread at loom; but what this change is, and how accomplished, I must defer to another communication, as I do not wish to take up too much space in your valuable paper."

It can be seen from the general tone of the letter all was not well in the weaving community. Indeed it was written the very year that the Weavers Society in the town was dissolved.

The demise of the weavers in Crieff followed the pattern elsewhere although interpretation of the available statistics gleaned from the census returns does indicate that as a group they held on here rather longer than elsewhere in the country. It was however a combination of market forces and cheaper alternatives that drove the final nail into the coffin. They had in the early 1800s held out for an improved pay structure which the existing "closed shop" guarded fiercely through the various Guilds or Societies. This had led to violence and combined with the Chartist agitation and support amongst their fraternity serious confrontation with authority. The serious of their plight can clearly be seen by reference to **Figure 1**. In the decade between 1841 and 1851 the number of weavers in Scotland dropped dramatically from 84 560 to 25 000. *The Perthshire Courier* of December 1839 claimed that number of webs that had arrived from Glasgow have been very limited that it is nearly impossible for the working man to earn a bare existence. One month later in January 1840 the same paper remarked that *"the state of weaving in Crieff is low at present. Very few webs have arrived from Glasgow for a number of weeks back and the consequence is that a great number of individuals are out of employment many of whom have large families and have had nothing to do for some weeks past and as little prospect for some weeks to come. What makes the case more distressing is that no outdoor labour can be procured at this time of year. We believe that if it was not owing to a number of individuals having still a few potatoes on hand many would be bordering on actual starvation."*

The Crieff Society staggered on until 1857 when on March 28th of that year the *Crieff Herald and Strathearn Advertiser* ran the following about the eventual end of the Society. *"The Society was formally dissolved on Monday last. The house property of the Society was disposed of last summer and the funds arising from that and other sources amounted to nearly five hundred pounds. This sum was distributed amongst the members in proportion to the length of time which each had been connected with the Society in shares ranging from 10/- up to £7.10s. These dividends have come very opportune to many poor persons in this inclement and dear season. As usual on such occasions there are a good many disputes some of which may require legal proceedings before they are rectified and there have been rather too many instances in which the dividend has proved but a questionable benefit."*

Crieff as we have mentioned sustained a weaving industry for a longer period than other similar places. On the 30th of September 1879 *The Perthshire Courier* had a head line *"Depression Of The Handloom Weaving Trade"*. It declared that *"three quarters of those engaged in this branch of the industry (the principal trade of the place) are out of employment. About the 4th of the month there were only 6 or 8 looms working and since that time only 34 webs have been received from Auchterarder* (the principal source of supply) *and a few short webs from Perth. These are all pretty high wrought out and it is extremely doubtful whether any more can be had from Auchterarder as the Messrs Halley are almost out of orders; and it is said that should the firm not be fortunate in securing further orders they intend to close their premises for some time. The village is ill enough at present for want of employment but since this fountain of supply ceased, it is indeed dismal to contemplate what must be the result."*

A little over a decade later it was virtually dead. Thus ended a chapter of rapid success and equally sudden failure. Sadly the memories of this unique band of individuals has virtually been expunged from our ken. They were quite unique those *"gallant weavers"*.

Chapter 5

THE CRIEFF TRYST

Background

Like most Scottish country towns or large villages, Crieff in the centre of Strathearn had a number of big occasions when the local populace gathered together to meet, celebrate and perhaps buy essentials for a future day. The principal day in the town was known as the Michaelmas Market. Originally, it dated back to the early charters granted to the Barony of Drummond. It was not just a time for locals to trade and barter, but a cattle market that continued to grow in importance throughout Scotland and indeed further afield in England. The Market or Tryst (meeting place) came into prominence in the early 1700s until it was transferred in 1770 to Falkirk by the Commissioners of the Forfeited Estates.

The location of the actual Tryst is not clear. According to Porteous "The Tryst was held on the southern and western slopes of the Knock" (p. 235). It is evident that despite the transfer to Falkirk, the Michaelmas Market continued on into the twentieth century. Porteous (p. 239) wrote in 1912 the following: *"Michaelmas Market though shorn of its former glory is still considered the principal one in Crieff. At one time the crowd attending it extended from what is now the Crown Hotel to Comrie Street and from James Square down to the Market Park. To a great extent it held its former reputation as a cattle market, the cattle being gathered together in the Market Park. All sorts of goods were for sale including boots, shoes, cloth, tin ware, pails and tubs while apple and pear carts and sweetie stands abounded. In addition, at this, as well as other markets, there were shows of different kinds, exhibiting giants or dwarfs or other freaks which were usually well patronised as were also merry go rounds, jugglers and cheap jacks."*

Why Crieff ?

The early cattle markets were scattered throughout Scotland. In 1669 all export and import duties that had existed between Scotland and England were abolished and in 1680 a Commission was set up to encourage trade. James, Earl of Perth obtained by Act of Parliament in 1672 the right to a yearly fair and weekly market in Crieff. Crieff was chosen as the venue for mainly geographic reasons. The Sma 'Glen was the traditional route from the north whilst cattle from the north east (Aberdeenshire) came down Strath Tay or from Blairgowrie and Alyth converging at Dunkeld and heading west up Strath Bran to Amulree and down to Crieff. The large numbers from Argyll (including Kintyre) and the islands made their way by Rannoch Moor, Glen Dochart and Lochs Tay and Earn to Crieff. This coupled with easy access for the buyers from the south promoted the town. The "black cattle" (they were actually of various colours) required grazing all along the routes so the drove roads tended to miss out centres of population.

Mackey's Journey through Scotland published in 1723 recalls his visit to the Tryst. There were then 30 000 beasts being sold for 30 000 guineas. The highland drovers often continued southwards offering their services to the dealers for one shilling a day for the southern trip and returning at their own expense.

What was it like?

The Market was held in the second week of October. It was under the control and patronage of the Earl of Perth who held a Court for the purpose of regulating disputes and keeping order. It was common for his feuars (i.e. those who held property on the Drummond Estate lands) to have an obligation to act as guards and police the market. According to the school master for Monzie in the Statistical Account of 1793 the good citizens of that Parish *"went in fear of their lives from the Highland drovers who broke into their houses, forcibly billeting themselves and often carried off part of the house hold goods and removed the potatoes from their fields"*. The Account for Crieff, written some 20 years after the demise of the Tryst, adopts a somewhat different approach: *"The old people here sometimes speak with deep regret of the glorious scene displayed to view when 30 000 black cattle in different droves overspread the whole adjacent country for several miles round the town."*

According to Haldane in *The Drove Roads of Scotland*, the Earl of Perth was entitled to levy " market dues " amounting to two pence a beast. He apparently "let" this right to one of his tenants for the yearly sum of £ 600 Scots which was some £50 sterling.

Much of the trade was done by means of bills and during the second quarter of the 18th century Crieff came to be regarded as one of the main financial centres of Scotland. Considerable sums changed hands in the form of gold and an entry in the *Minute Book of the Royal Bank of Scotland* in 1730 shows that tellers were that year sent from Edinburgh to Crieff with £3 000 in notes to put into circulation in return for cash.

Why the move to Falkirk?

Falkirk was more accessible for buyers from the south but the chief reason for the change lay in the importance to drovers reaching the market from the North by the easiest and quickest routes. According to the Statistical Account for Crieff for 1794, *"the drovers from Argyll, Inverness and Ross shire paid nothing for pasturing their cattle on the way to the market; but in the improved state of the country, grass became more valuable, the roads more confined and the drovers were forced to enquire after the most convenient and cheap roads from their several homes to the principal market place now at Falkirk, where the roads leading by the shortest course from every quarter of the Highlands towards England naturally unite."*

By the last decade of the 18th century, the cattle coming down the Sma' Glen by passed the town the day before the date fixed for the Tryst thus avoiding the market dues which were still levied. The cattle crossed the Earn at Dalpatrick Ford on a direct line from Gilmerton at the end of Sma' Glen Road. The name Highlandman is a relic of those days. The drove then headed for Muthill (Highlandman Park) and over the Orchil to Greenloaning and Sheriffmuir (where there was common grazing) to Bridge of Allan and the valley of the Forth on to Falkirk. Some of the cattle went via Glen Devon and the Ochils. Sadly for Crieff and for the Strath, the high days of the Tryst were well and truly over.

Chapter 6

Roads and Railways in the Strath

The Roman occupation of Strathearn probably saw the construction of the first recognizable road system as the occupants in their established tradition built a road system to enable communication between their various outposts. The road over the Langside from Braco to Comrie connected the main camp at Ardoch with the Dalginross "glen blocker". The Gask Ridge represented a frontier of forts and watchtowers stretching from Ardoch to Bertha at modern Inveralmond. The Romans constructed a military road to connect these various posts and these have been excavated as part of ongoing research under Dr DW Woolliscroft and a team of archaeologists from Liverpool University. Various excavations have been carried out to determine how these roads were constructed. Although construction techniques may have varied dependent on the location, the Parkneuk and Roundlaw sections of the Gask road indicated that the Romans laid turves over the existing ground and made up the foundations in hardcore stones from a local source. The road was between 20 and 24 feet (some 7.25 metres) wide and laid to a camber and blinded on the surface with gravel. At Roundlaw the existing farm road is thought to be the actual Roman road constructed all those centuries ago!

Tradition, nay legend, tells us that part of King Street in Crieff was a Roman way. It should be remembered of course that when they occupied Strathearn some 2000 years ago, Crieff as a town or village was not there. The straight lines of existing roads such as those from Muthill to Crieff (the A822) and the back road between Garrick Cottage and Muthill off the A822 and skirting the Muir of Orchill depict characteristics of the Roman road building ethos concerning the shortest way between two points! It may well have been the shallow ford across at Bridgend in Crieff that saw them choose this line as a way to their camp at Fendoch in the Sma' Glen.

As with the rest of Scotland, the departure of the Romans saw a deterioration of roads, which gradually became virtually unusable due to lack of maintenance. Porteous in his History of Crieff recounts a horrendous tale involving Lord Lovat on the aforementioned A822 (as it is now) in 1740. Making his way from Drummond Castle south towards Dunblane en route to Edinburgh from Inverness with his two daughters, he writes, "I got to

Drummond Castle where we were storm stayed by the most tempestuous weather of wind and rain I ever remember. Setting forth eventually, I was not three miles gone from the castle when the axle-tree of my fore wheels broke in two in the midst of the hill betwixt Drummond and the Bridge of Ardoch, and we were forced to sit in the hill with a boisterous day till Chamberlain Drummond was so kind as to go down the Strath and bring wrights, carts and smiths to our assistance who dragged us to the plain, where we were forced to stay five or six hours till there was a new axle-tree made, so that it was dark night before we came to Dunblane, which is but eight miles from Castle Drummond all much fatigued. Eventually we reached Edinburgh in safety, having taken eleven days for the journey".

Lord Fraser and his daughters' experiences give vivid insight to the condition of the roads of the period. In an effort to remedy the situation, the government passed a number of Turnpike or Statute Labour laws which

Comrie suffered severe flooding in the 1990s but things were as bad in 1910.

FLOOD IN DALGINROSS, COMRIE

were an attempt to enforce able bodied men to carry out six days of manual labour on the roads each year. In Strathearn, the results were somewhat mixed. Local Justices of the Peace administered the Acts enforcing individuals to carry out the work. As the statutory registration of births, marriages and deaths did not come in to being in Scotland until the 1st of January 1855, they could not have had a formal list of people who were being requested to carry out the hard labour of the "Parish Road Days". The existing old parish registers covering Crieff were not obligatory and only started in the 1690s. This period did however see the construction of two roads to Perth, the first being that via what is now Dollerie Terrace and the second by Highlandman. Porteous's account gives a lot of interesting detail regarding the road construction in the mid 18th century. As the labour to be used was not voluntary or indeed by choice, the numbers turning out was disappointing. Mr Thomas Caw, know locally as the "Provost", was appointed overseer for the task with the assistance of one John Galloway, the local constable .The Local Justices issued them with the following: "You are hereby ordered to call out the inhabitants of the Parish of Crieff, according to lists to be given to you, and on the days appointed by Mr Thomas Caw, overseer for that road, and you are to intimate to all those you call out to work upon that road, the penalties of the law in case they delay, or refuse to come to the roads when commanded thereto; and as there is another road intended on the north of the Pow, you are to summon such of the town and parish to the south road as live on the south side of the street or great road going through Crieff from east to west, and such of the tenants as live on the south side of the present road leading from Crieff to Corrievechter Easter and Dollerie, and leave the others on the north thereof to assist at the north road. (The 'present road' above mentioned is the old road by Kincardine.)"

Despite the somewhat threatening attitude to the citizens of the town, work on the projects would appear to have progressed at a snail's pace. Such was the dissatisfaction amongst the Justices and the local lairds that a meeting was convened in Crieff in 1742 to determine what steps should be taken to expedite matters. The Duke of Perth was prominent amongst the latter and the various proprietors along the routes to Perth were given the task of directing operations over that part passing through their lands. The meeting issued the following statement: "The inhabitants of Crieff have shown an unwillingness to go to the making of the road and have made but small progress considering the numbers who have gone out, that it be made optional for the inhabitants to go out three days this summer or pay 12 shillings Scots on or before 10th May next". A fine of 20 shillings Scots was to be levied on defaulters and instructions were given to Thomas Caw to draw up a fresh list of those liable to work, while fourteen who had failed in their duty were to be summoned to attend a meeting of the justices. The tools purchased by public monies to construct the road were to be passed on to the next proprietor as the work was completed on the foregoing stage. About 1790 the road now called the Perth Road, starting from the east end of High Street, was formed. It joined the old Perth Road near Callum's Hill.

The unsatisfactory nature of the system to construct a new road network was soon recognised as subsequent Acts amended the situation. A levy or tax superseded the statutory labour requirement and a rate of 1/6 (7.5 pence) was imposed after 1751. By the end of the 18th century the Turnpike Acts introduced tolls on the new roads and tollhouses were set up to gather the revenue. In Crieff six were built, two at Bridgend, two at Dalvreck and two at "Charing Cross", the guschet between Dollerie Terrace, Perth Road and East High Street. Of all the tollhouses only these last two remain having been renovated by J & R Robertson, local building contractors around 1980 and transformed into a pleasant single residence. During the renovations when the wall linings were stripped back, it became clear what the original lay out had been. The present Perth Road is much higher than at the time of the tolls. A window on the north wall had been built up and was some two metres below the present street level. This part of the property was the tollhouse dealing with traffic on the main highway to Perth whilst the southern part was the one serving the Gleneagles Turnpike.

We have examined elsewhere in this narrative the road building exploits of General Wade in Strathearn and north of the Sma' Glen. His road system dates from the period after the Jacobite Uprising of 1714 from about 1725. His road started from the Bridgend in Crieff, up King Street and over Ferntower. His construction methods have proven incredibly similar to those of the Roman occupants of the first century AD. Although many of his bridges have long since gone, some remain including a superb little one over a burn near Newton and of course the magnificent one at Aberfeldy which

The toll house erected at "Charing Cross", Crieff, the guschet between the Gleneagles turnpike (now Dollerie Terrace) and the Perth Road. Built around the end of the 18th century it was renovated in the 1980s.

is still in use. It was built by Wade but designed by the architect William Adam. Before we leave the subject of bridges, mention should be made of the "Roman" bridge at Monzie. The appended Edwardian post card was of a much-photographed scene at the old mill of Monzie (see page 66). Whether or not it was actually built by the Romans is a matter of great scepticism. Its rustic rubble construction is similar to a number of bridges in the Strathearn area including the one over the Barvick some four miles to the west.

One benefit achieved by the construction of the new roads was that for the first time the towns and villages were at last within reasonable reach of the principal towns and cities of Scotland. Apart from the horses and carts of public carriers plying regular routes bringing and taking wares to Strathearn, a number of stagecoach services were introduced. Crieff became a post town with the Glasgow to Perth mail coach being routed through its congested streets. It must have been an exciting scene as the daily coach and horses galloped in via the narrow approach of Duchlage Road, which was, until 1823, the main access from the south. Before long Crieff was also being served by the Edinburgh mail coach as well as a number of services for the public allowing at last access to the outside world. Coaches such as the Comrie Dasher, The Strathearn Lass, Bessie Bell, Mary Gray, The Victor and the Rapid plied their routes between the towns and villages of the Strath. There even was a "lawyers' coach" laid on to transport Crieff's solicitors to the county town and legal metropolis of Perth!

In 1820, Robert Stevenson, grand father of the author Robert Louis Stevenson, presented a "memorial", or in modern parlance, a feasibility study to a number of eminent personages including His Grace the Duke of Atholl, the Right Honourable the Earl of Strathmore, the Honourable W.R. Maule, M.P., James Wemyss, Esq. Younger of Wemyss, M.P. and the other noblemen, gentlemen and magistrates. This memorial was "regarding the propriety of opening the great valleys of Strathmore and Strathearn, by means of a railway or canal". The presentation included a hand coloured folding, engraved map, with blue printed wrappers. It outlined plans to connect Perth, at the head of the Tay navigation system, with towns both east and west. Canals were to be constructed through both Strathmore and Strathearn. It had been discussed since the middle of the 18th century and indeed Stevenson himself had reported on a Strathmore canal in 1817. Here he shows why the country would be suitable either for canal or railway, before coming down in favour of horse-drawn edge railways, describing the advantage of such a system over both canals and roads.

Things however were changing rapidly and after the economic depression following the Napoleonic Wars, things improved dramatically. Bumper crops in 1842 and 1843 heralded an improving affluence in the country. The stock market was awash with spare cash ripe for investment and the prospect of good returns from investment in the newly invented railway system was proving popular. In 1844 there were some 66 proposed railway construction bills before Parliament. Local persons of influence felt that Perth and Strathearn, to the west, should be part of this rapidly expanding network, which was gradually spreading out its lines throughout these isles. The ground had been surveyed in 1841 and by 1844 a Committee for the Railway from Perth by Stirling to the Edinburgh and Glasgow Railway had been duly formed under the chairmanship of Charles Sidey, Lord Provost of Perth. The number of influential landowners in the area who became involved was substantial. Amongst them were Laurence Oliphant of Condie who was a former MP for Perth City, HL Colquhoun of Clathick and Archibald Turnbull of Bellwood. The initial meeting heard a proposal from John Campbell, 2nd Marquis of Breadalbane urging that a prospectus be issued for the construction of a railway from Perth to a junction with Edinburgh and Glasgow Railway near Falkirk. Indeed this followed on soon

Crieff station showing looking west taken in the summer of 1954.

afterwards on the 15th of March as a result of a high powered gathering in Edinburgh attended by, amongst others, the Marquis, Lord Kinnaird, joint promoter of the adjoining Dundee and Perth Railway, Sir Patrick Murray Threipland of the Carse of Gowrie and John Stirling of Kippendavie near Dunblane. Without much ado a provisional committee was set up and things began to move.

Named the Scottish Central Railway, the subscribers initiated a detailed engineering survey together with an estimate of cost. This was carried out by the Mitchell family from Inverness who had a well-established pedigree in railway and canal construction. After much consideration as to the actual route to be followed, the Company came down in favour of the route by tunnel through Moncrieff Hill and on into Perth town. The alternative choice before them was to swing north from Auchterarder towards Crieff and thence following the line of the Pow Burn into Perth. Undoubtedly if this choice had been followed it would have had great economic benefits for Crieff as the proposal would have virtually by passed Perth to link up with the Strathmore line to the north. Perth would have ended up at the end of a branch line, something its worthy citizens would not have welcomed.

Proposals followed that a branch lined would be formed to connect Crieff to the main SCR line at Greenloaning. Unfortunately financial constraints put paid to that scheme which had suggested initially that when the main line opened in 1848, the Crieff connection would also have been completed. Some five years later things had moved on a pace and the Crieff Junction Railway Bill received Parliamentary and Royal Assent on the 15th of August 1853. The engineer appointed by the company to be responsible for all aspects of design and construction was a man who had established a reputation for building cheap railways throughout Scotland. That man was Thomas Bouche. Bouche (later Sir Thomas Bouche) was the person who designed and took responsibility for the ill-fated Tay Rail Bridge. That disaster in 1879 virtually killed the man who had at the time had been working on his Forth Bridge project.

The Crieff project suffered dreadful delays and set backs despite an optimistic opening date from the contractor, James Gowans. On reflection many of the reasons for delays lay with Bouche who had taken on too many other projects and failed to devote the necessary time and consideration to the job in hand. The intentions were that the SCR would actual operate the smaller Crieff Junction Railway providing the necessary locomotives and carriages. Staff employed by the CJR for the proposed opening had to be paid off when it became clear that completion of the line could not meet the date. As many of those had been in the previous employ of the larger company, feelings between the two were not good. The opening date of the 13th March 1856 proved yet another disappointment as the Central refused to permit its locomotive to pass over the track work at Crieff Junction Station to the east of Green loaning (later to be called Gleneagles) as it was deemed to be unsatisfactory. After consultation between Gowans and the Central's engineer, modifications were carried out to the track and, a day late, the line opened.

There appears to have been considerable bad feeling between the two Companies and it was only some nine years later that this ceased when the two amalgamated.

In 1864, the Crieff and Methven Junction Railway was established and after meeting held in the Drummond Arms Crieff, work was sanctioned. Once again delays followed and eventually it opened to the public in 1866. The following poem quoted by Porteous and written by a Mr John C Fisher, a native of Crieff sums the opening of the line in a most apposite manner. As a song it was sung to the tune of *Bonnie Dundee*!

Crieff station showing looking east taken in the summer of 1954.

We hae gotten a start in the richt way at last
For commerce and railways are multiplin' fast
And soon from our home in the North we can ride
To the banks of the Tay, the Forth or the Clyde

The gude folks o' Crieff deserve noo a sang
For a nice thriving place they'll mak' it ere lang
Wi' railways, and Baillies , a Provost , and a ' —
Us Crieff folks, ye see, are getting 'fu' braw .

Since the Crieff and Methven line's first turf is cut
There's gladness in many a hamlet and hut, —
And may anxious bit wish for the day
When an engine shall puff on the Methven Railway .

The lady we thank here , who opened this line
And all who joined the procession so fine
Our Provost, the Masons, and Crieff Volunteers ,
Let's gie them, dear friends, three loud ringin' cheers .

On the opening day, the 21st of May 1866, it was declared a holiday in Crieff. Three trains departed that morning with an incredible crowd on board of nearly 1 000 passengers.

The development in a westerly direction out of Crieff was somewhat slow in happening. Efforts fronted by Comrie proprietor Colonel Williamson of Lawers came to little. Opposition came from Crieff Town Council when it was revealed that the line would cut through the Town Green known as the Meadow. This area, a former bleaching field had been the subject of earlier discussion when an ownership issue arose. The site of this controversy is now occupied by the Somerfield supermarket. At last Comrie was joined to Crieff when the first train puffed out on the 1st of June 1893 at 6.30 am.

The final link in the chain was connecting Comrie to Lochearnhead. This most scenic of routes traversed the north side of Loch Earn finally entering Lochearnhead and then dipping southwards to Balquhidder Junction where it joined up with the Callander and Oban railway. The line was authorised in 1897 and opened shortly after this. The Balquhidder end had a single timber shed with a 60' turntable. The Lochearnhead station is now a Boy Scout Centre located behind the former Lochearnhead Hotel. The lines were absorbed by the Caledonian Railway in 1902.

What happened?

Railways were an important part of life for more than 100 years. In Strathearn, Dr Beeching's savage cuts of the 1960s saw the demise of what had been a way of life. The railways in Strathearn were major employees. Analysis of figures in the census books of the late 19th century shows that railways were at one time the second largest employers in the area. The axe fell and it was no more!

The complexity of the Crieff railway set up is best appreciated by examination of the ordnance survey map of 1902. Two lines approached Crieff from the east. The areas above Duchlage Farm comprised cattle pens, a saw mill (where the Duchlage Court now exists), a timber yard, an engine shed, sidings and a water tank. The lines then passed under Duchlage Road and split into numerous sidings, peripheral to the main station. Apart from coal depots, there were three sawmills, a timber yard and various small buildings. The station had two platforms with glass canopies. An attempt to run rail busses where you could flag down a "bus" at certain spots proved a failure. The line closed in 1964 and the land lay derelict for a number of years. I can recall walking Murphy my pet pooch in the shrubbery that was once the station yard. Platforms were clearly discernible and the ground had a high ash content! For a while a bike track utilised the space once occupied by holidaymakers and Crieff businessmen heading for the opportunistic offices of Stirling and Perth. Now the site comprises sheltered housing (Duchlage), a small industrial estate, the new cottage hospital, the new (2000) Crieff Health Centre and its currently empty predecessor! The embankment over Morrison's Academy 's playing fields at Dallerie has been excavated away to provide up fill for new roads to the new houses now occupied by Strathearn's latest occupants. The bridge over the Turrett has gone. The line of the railway as it makes its tortuous way westwards is obscured with newly sprouted greenery and its undergrowth provides nature with a more acceptable habitat. Have things really changed?

Chapter 7

Strathearn in the early Victorian period

A bit of this and a piece of that!

NB The following appeared in a publication dated 1897 called *Crieff in the Victorian Era* published by H.K. Brown of 15 King Street, Crieff.

A lovely cloud of dust, not of the crushed metal order, has its being somewhere about those parts of South Bridgend where at present a prosperous jamary holds sway; and sweeping over the bridge before a delightful summer' s breeze, curls and circles in the air and forms into any number of fantastic looking shapes, the favourite representation being the ponderous bows of the old Norse warship. Before the breeze has lost its playful influence the dust reaches the Gallowhill, where it feels the want of sufficient encouragement and drops dead opposite somebody's door. The track of the phantom can be followed if one cares to do so, and if anyone wants to take a different route, he may by slipping off his shoes and stockings and rolling up his trousers wade the Earn, and arrive at any desired destination on the others side, without let or hindrance. But in this (past) age of achievement and advancement people hold no very decided superstition about the bridge though it looks as unstable as a dromedary in a travelling menagerie, and the usual custom is not to wade through the water, but to go across the river in the manner common to the later day pedestrians.* When one reaches the north side of the bridge and takes a step or two up the hill he finds he has got at last to Crieff. I say at last, as anyone not acquainted with the place may not know exactly when he is in or out of it. Scattered here and there, in various shapes and sizes, and facing in all directions, are a few thatched houses. Some face north and some south; some are ends north and south, while others are due east and west. There is

*It may be mentioned that the bridge referred to was rather a deformed looking arrangement. Local historians of more or less importance have endeavoured to solve the question of its deformity, but in giving a satisfactory answer they have all ignominiously failed. The fact is that the disfigurement was caused by a big Comrie earthquake, which took place many years ago, before reporting became extraordinary and before the extent of the upheavals was measured by the wavy movement of liquid ink in the office of the senior magistrate. The present bridge over the Earn was built in 1868.

no interfering Dean of Guild Court to instruct the peaceful householders as to what is regular or irregular, or to direct them in the law regarding oriels; so they fix their windows and doors where and how they please and consult no one as to whether they have done right or wrong. Here, indeed the flag of freedom waves triumphantly. On the street side the grass grows for the benefit of about a dozen cows, and all manner of wild flowers prosper in abundance.

The seeds from this wayside paradise flit hither and thither as the prevailing winds direct, and when you see a fair exhibition of the cottage garden on the thatched roof you know that Nature has been exceedingly kind in presenting her beauties unsolicited.

Up near the chimneys which have their faces delightfully coloured with soot generated from the fumes of Auchnafree peats, dandelions and poppies rear their heads side by side with buttercups and bluebells, while along the rigging grass grows in a healthy form competing each year from the highest blades. Somewhere about the gables, from which the rain has been running in streams onto the kitchen floor, the spaces are closely turfed, and heavy stones are added to keep the wind from doing further damage. If the cow is at all a cleanly beast sometimes whether it is or not it is permitted to hang its hat on the door "ben the hoose", and to bellow at its convenience; but generally speaking, the animal is apportioned a room at the back, with a "through" entrance from the kitchen. The family pig a lower animal for reasons which need not be stated, is allotted a separate house in the yard, and there it grunts the livelong day as it stares between the gaping spars at the green kail which grows temptingly outside. Sometimes it raises itself on its hind legs with the usual grace, and looks over the top spar to admire the scenery and general crops in the garden. The trough, however slips out from below, and as the beast falls back with a semi summersault into three feet of filth, an extra special grunt is forthcoming by way of expressing its contempt for "sour grapes". Further up the street you are in a nobbier community. A clay pipe and a few samples of groceries denote a merchant's shop, and if you find a shoe or two in a window you know that this is a shoemakers. Here there is some attempt at decoration. The holes in the window panes are padded up with old shirts and trousers, red creepers try to climb the doorposts, and a bull finch chirps at the outer door. Up the street you may see the two neighbour women in close confab as they meet at the well; down the street you may see some children playing with the dust; here and there dogs lie basking in the sun; and occasionally a busy weaver appears at his door to note the progress of the sun on its journey westward. Further up the hill there are a few better class houses. You know what that means. The addition of a chimney pot in a falling condition, and a sneck on the door which works every sixth trial. There is also an effort at white washing. Here, then, is Crieff, in which prosper a noble class of worthy and contented weavers, whose sons may live to see their families grow up brilliant scholars, or to learn of their success as highly intelligent poachers.

Crieff's Prison

As it was in 1837

The Town Hall in the centre of Crieff today houses the Tourist Information Office whilst upstairs in the old Burgh Chambers the present Community Council hold their monthly sessions. In 1999 the basement rooms were upgraded and in what was in the 19th century the town jail, there now is on display the refurbished relics of thee old town including the Jougs or stocks, the Market Cross and the Strowan Cross. The soft lighting and the fresh decor is a world apart from what it was like many decades ago. This exert from the long defunct Perthshire Courier appeared in October 1837 and paints a grim picture of the state of the towns "lock up" at that time. William IV had just died and the young Victoria had not yet been crowned.

Mr Hill's report on the Prison of Crieff

The prison of Crieff is used as a lock up house only. It consists of a single cell 20' long, 15' broad and 8' high on a level with the street, and under a room formerly used as a guard house. The prison is old and insecure. The last instance of an escape occurred about 4 years ago. There being only one room, males and females are sometimes confined together; occasionally, however, when the offence is trifling, the female is set at liberty to avoid this evil. The prison is tolerably dry and moderately ventilated. There are no means of warming it, however, and in winter it must be very cold. I found the place in rather a slovenly state, there being a heap of coals in it. There was no prisoner at the time of my visit. I was told, however, that there are on average at least three or four every week, and that there would be many more if there were proper accommodation. At present all offenders sentenced to confinement, however short the period, must be sent to Perth, a distance of 17 miles. Many of the prisoners are deserters. There is no provision for feeding the prisoners, although they sometimes remain a whole day in confinement. It appears, however, that the gaoler gives them some food himself, for which he is sometimes, though not always, paid by the burgh. The bedding consists of a straw mattress, 2 blankets and a pillow. The blankets are washed once a year .The gaoler looks like a respectable man, and is apparently well qualified for his duties. The prison is under the jurisdiction of the county justices of the peace.

State of Crime at Crieff. There appears to be a great deal of crime here, consisting chiefly of thefts and assaults. Among the thefts, stealing poultry is particularly common. Very many of the offences escape detection. The amount of crime is said to be on the increase; which is partly accounted for by the great extent of drunkenness in the town. There are 27 males and 15 females in Crieff, who are looked upon as habitual offenders; namely, 9 males who steal and commit assaults (7 of whom poach also;) 14 who poach and commit assaults and who are suspected of stealing also; and 4 who poach but do not commit any other offences. All of these are between 16 and 30 years old. Of the females, 13 are thieves, and are between the ages of 16 and 32; and 2 (from 50 to 60 years old) are receivers of stolen goods. All these offenders are reported to be "great drinkers of ardent spirits." Many of the offenders commence their career by poaching. The parents are generally as bad as themselves. Most of the offences are committed by resident inhabitants, though many are committed by vagrants and high-landers who have been turned out of their crofts and who have obtained a settlement in the town.

State of the Police: Quite inefficient. The only man on duty is one hired to look after vagrants. Before he was appointed (6 years ago) the town was overrun by beggars, many of them sturdy ones. Two or three resident justices of the peace are much wanted. The procurator fiscal is at present often obliged to send 3 miles to get a warrant signed for the apprehension of an offender.

James Square

The Crieff Square Well

Have ye stood by the lime tree that grows in the square?
The old square of Crieff that spot ever fair
Where the glories of day show the Strath so sublime
And the night dew falls there on the beautiful lime.
The beautiful lime trees so gnarled and old
That for ages have stood in the sunshine and cold!
How blessed is the spot where its broad shadow fell
That fountain of fountains, the Crieff Square Well.

The Crieff Square Well, where the maidens so fair
May be seen with their pails by the trees in the square
With eyes like the diamond, so brightly they shine
And their light step so graceful – so seemingly divine
Who could forget them though far from the square
On some foreign shore, never more to be there?
But their thoughts they must wander, wherever the dwell
To the scenes of their youth by the Crieff Square Well.

Thou dear Square Well in the village of Crieff
What rapture when near thee – to leave thee what grief!
What flood of old memories come surging when there
By the old grey well, and the trees in the square!
As we stand by the well, in the evening alone

And muse on the natives departed and gone
We feel in that spot as if held by some spell
Under the lime trees, by the Crieff Square Well.

When the armies of Britain, in Egypt and Spain
Drove the baffled invaders full oft o'er the plain
When Napoleon the grand scowl'd black on our isle
As we grappled his power on the Tagus and Nile
And long was the struggle when gallant Moore bled
And Graham at Borossa his brave heroes led
Where some of that band who fought and who fell
Babbled in death of the Crieff Square Well.

Another day closed and the battle was done
And Wellington slept on the field he had won

And the watch fires burned low where the sentinel trod
By the dying and dead on the blood crimsoned sod
And a sad murmuring voice he listened to hear
As a poor dying comrade he chanced to come near
Mangled and gory with splinters of shell
Oh water, he said, from the Crieff Square Well.
With life ebbing fast far away into Spain
His thoughts wandered back to the village again
Though the world forever was leaving his view

The last throb of his heart to Crieff it beat true
Cold then he lay on his foes' bloody track
Where the columns of Gaul were they hurled back;
Where charging that Crieff youth, in glory he fell
Thirsting in death for the Crieff Square Well

Where is the villager – breathe not his name:
It would crimson the cheek with feelings of shame –
Who the dear village could ever forget,
Where his days they be spent, or his lot it be set?
What Crieff man forgets the old village square?
Where in days of his youth he attended the fair,
And the showman around of their wonders did tell,
By the old linden trees and the Crieff Square Well?

Some towns may have fountains more graceful to see,
But the Square Well of Crieff is the fountain for me.

How pure is its water, in summer how cold –
Delightful to taste, with virtues untold!
Then guard well the fountain that stands in the square,
For where is the fountain so rich or so rare?
Oh, where is the fountain will ever excel
That purest of fountains, the Crieff Square Well?

The Square now is not the Square of yesterday and indeed the old Square

Well of past verse. The author of the above, one John McCulloch or "Barnkittock" (an apt Strathearn nom de plume) as he was better known as, is largely forgotten. The Square itself has undergone countless changes. Gone are the lime trees and indeed the Square Well itself. The original James Square, named after James Drummond, third Duke of Perth has been erroneously referred to in past in sundry journals as "St James Square" a somewhat belated blessing on one of the Strath's oldest families and their Episcopal and Catholic past! Indeed the original Square was designed by an antecedent one Sir George Drummond of Milnab who amongst other attainments rose to be Lord Provost of Edinburgh. Although not traditionally the centre of the town (that honour lies eastwards at the Cross) the Square has since its inception been something of a focal point for citizens of Crieff. Banks and the Post office were to be found there from an early date together with the residencies of the town's more distinguished citizens. The Drummond Arms albeit disguised in traditional Crieff Victoriana architecture was a place of great importance. Old photographs show the original Drummond in its basic splendour on the corner with Hill Wynd (not street). The building was according to Porteous named the "Drummond of Perth's Arms, Tavern and Hotel" which would not have gone down well with the Commissioner's of the Forfeited Estates after the last Jacobite skirmish! It changed its name to the somewhat bland "Robertson's Inn" before reverting to the present "Drummond Arms". A popular place with Perthshire "gentry", it hosted numerous functions and "dancing assemblies" in its day. Its fame and attraction to the landed aristocracy of the time was no doubt attributable to a stay some years distant of the Young Pretender who convened a war cabinet in the fervent days of the last Jacobite uprising. Crieff's attitude to the Prince and his cause has been somewhat overlooked. Like most Scots the general feeling was ambivalent. Towns on the borders of the gaedhealteachd and the Lowlands were particularly edgy. Crieff was no different. The accounts of the "burnings" of the first Uprising have traditionally been recounted through the words of Presbyterian ministers and the qualifications of the Maitland Club papers published in the early days of the nineteenth century tend to portray a somewhat more balanced assessment. Chaired by the then Duke of Argyll whose ancestor led the Hanoverian forces at Sheriffmuir, they describe the reasoning behind the scorched earth policy adopted by Mar and condemn the now generally accepted but rather biased accounts of the minister's appraisal of the local scene. With hindsight it is clear that Crieff had more than a few citizens who followed their laird's example in siding with Charlie.

In a modern context, the Square has seen changes. Present memory recalls the draughts games where locals and visitors enjoyed combat with pole and chequer! Less salubrious were the subterranean former toilets which provided a secret haunt for the youth of the time! The present rehabilitation undertaken after much discussion met with a degree of opposition. Gone were the limes of Barnkittock's poem and gone too was the Square Well of past memory. In its place arose a new Square which even the most biased of citizens must surely now regard as a vast improvement. The somewhat continental layout and atmosphere has enabled the Square to return to its original function as a meeting place for all! The bands and choirs perform on a regular basis and attract audiences which in the past would have fore gathered at the under used band stand standing forlornly in the park! Still in its place is the fountain erected to the generosity of the Murrays of Ochtertyre in providing the town with an abundant supply of fresh water. But that of course is another story! Not to be overlooked are the commemorative lamp posts erected as tribute to Victoria and her consort on the occasion of her jubilee. One can but hope that in years to come the horrendous traffic problems thereabout can be sorted out and the Square can return to a semblance of the past. Indeed local bye laws have already eradicated not a few of the other human problems!

Antiquarian Discovery at Crieff

The following appeared in the *Dundee Advertiser* of the 4th April 1894.

"During recent removal of an old dwelling house at Croftnappock, a suburb of Crieff, the workman in digging up some flags found a peculiar carved stone measuring about 3 1/2 feet by 13 inches. The back and sides of the stone are rough hewn and it seems have been built into a wall or fixed in some place with other stones. Croftnappock means the abbot's croft and there is no doubt of the house and ground of about 6 acres attached having at a former time been an ecclesiastical possession. In the memory of old men a room or two in the house were used by the Parish Church for Session purposes. Mr Alexander Hutcheson has favoured us with the following remarks as to the age and ornamentation of the stone. This interesting stone is a fragment of a monument slab and bears along with the figure of the cross and other sculpturings, the name of the person commemorated. The cross belongs to the type known as Maltese, having equal arms with expanded ends; a four leaf flower is carved in the centre and the arms are thrown into relief and ornameted – the upper and lower by horizontal transverse bands, and the right and left limbs by concentric triangular panelling. The cross is continued downwards in a somewhat narrow shaft, diamonded by simple incised lines, while the spaces on either side of the shaft are occupied by designs in relief. The inscription occupies the upper part of the stone and is incomplete. It is in old English or ecclesiastical characters. Fragments of four lines remain which probably indicate a pre Reformation origin. A translated form reads 'Pray for the soul of Donald Makculloch (sic), who to his good memory caused this to be erected.' The sculpture and execution are rude and the stone probably belongs to the latter half of the 15th Century."

Cock Fighting in Strathearn

Today Crieff and indeed Strathearn as a whole are active on the sporting front. The towns and villages boast a great number of football teams covering all age groups and enjoying the tough competition of Perthshire's Amateur Leagues. Cricket although perhaps not quite as popular as it was, is still played in many of the towns and villages throughout the county. Rugby too is popular and draws a good support on regular occasions whilst bowls, curling and of course, golf are all-popular with all age groups.

As the 18th century drew to a close, local sportsman in Strathearn were very much in a different time warp! Country pursuits naturally were dominant and in Crieff and the surrounding villages cock fighting was sure to draw crowds which were well in excess of present day numbers at a football match in the Market Park! Despite the apparent popularity of the "sport", the Weavers Guild of Crieff in 1820 thought otherwise when they passed a resolution concerning their premises in what is now Commissioner Street "that all cockers be excluded from entering the hall with fighting cocks". Some nine years later this ban was extended to "badger baiters or any other games that excite cruelty". In England and Wales cock fighting was banned in 1835 but in Scotland was legal up until 1895.

In 1837, the year of Queen Victoria's coronation, there was held a cock fight on the Broich Estate just south of the town. The following account is one of the few remaining which describe the popularity the sport had in Strathearn. Like modern horse racing, cock fighting attracted the gamblers, which perhaps explains why it held such an interest for the citizens of the Strath.

"Good Queen Victoria the first is coronated. The bell rings, the folks cheer and do may other things necessary for the occasion, and the day passes amidst very satisfactory enthusiasm. But there is something which remains to complete the day, and that something is on everybody's mind. It is a cock fight. To witness the encounter Lochlane, Strowan, and Monzievaird. Fowlis and Monzie send their hordes, who come mainly in hay carts.

For days past the young Queen and the cock fight have been discussed and re discussed in every weaver's shop, at every corner, at every farm, and on every road, and the money at stake being in proportion to the importance of the event, the names of the principal sportsmen are upon everybody's lips. All the country roads swarm with the heavy traffic, and the people stager forward in their hurry to reach the town. Carts, with their precious loads, rumble along; farmers on horseback mingle with the crowd; and the cries and shouts of the passengers make the merry clanking of the harness on the excited horses almost sink into insignificance. 'The Young Queen', 'Horrah, Horrah,' and the cries are kept up for miles along the road – only to be repeated and passed back with additional enthusiasm. Everywhere friendship and good fellowship prevail in honour of the great day. Before the sun sets a fight unparalleled in interest for miles around will be fought and won.

King and Sharp have long held names notorious for cock fighting. The former – the owner of many gallant birds – belongs the Bridgend, and in an honest, open fight can produce birds to match anything in the district. The challenge was thrown out by Sharp of Crieff, whose shady practices were not by any means unfamiliar to the ring, but whose name as a cunning breeder of first class birds was well and widely known. Both finely-trained smugglers, they had fallen out in a public house near Amulree, and after the fight was announced and the stakes were arranged, the news was spread about in all directions. It required no sporting newspaper then to intimate coming events.

A beautiful site for the encounter has been selected on the Broich Estate {the belief is that the Laird is ill in bed}. And what a glorious afternoon! A cloudless sky extends from the Grampians to the Ochils, and the sinking sun shines forth in all its lurid glory; the gentle wind familiar to June sighs peacefully in every tree, and the roads are carpeted with the dust of many days. As the last rays of the sun strike upon the valley the enormous crowd begin to wend their way in the direction of the Bridge; and, crossing the burn by a series of planks fixed for the occasion, are soon in the neighbourhood of the ring. Closely they pack together, and those who are late in arriving fill up the open space on the hillock behind which a splendid view of the ring can be obtained. How many people there will be present it is difficult to estimate. But they form a mixed crowd. From every part of the district representatives are present, and conversation is loud and vigorous on the prospects of the coming fight. Monzie men support Sharp because his mother is a McAra; the Strowan contingent back King because his sister is married to the Laird's coachman; while the Fowlis men, actuated by the same motives which impelled the Ephesian idolmakers to shout 'Great is Dianna' &c., range themselves on the side of Sharp {Fowlis at this time was the chief centre of the riddle making industry, and King being engaged in this trade in the Bridgend the position of the Fowlis men easily understood}. The Muthill representatives again stick fast to the Crieff man because of an old-standing feud with the Bridgend.

Here in this mighty throng what excitement prevails? The spectators behind press forward; those in front press back, and the people roar and cheer as the names of favourite sportsmen are shouted across the ring. Good-humoured banter passes between the men of Fowlis and Bridgend – the latter indulging in trade references regarding the 'Celestial City' and riddle trade. Monzie and Monzievaird remind each other of past tussles in the ring and the hour for the start comes quickly upon them. As final preparations are being made by the referee, shouts of 'The Broich', 'The Broich', are heard from the top of the hillock, at that moment the Laird, who is a terror to the whole community, is seen striding over the turnip field in the vicinity of the arena. The two principals secure their birds, and make their escape; the referee remembering the fate of the old poacher, and knowing the dangers of entering the Broich preserves, takes to his heels, and the whole crowd follow suit at their utmost speed towards the public highway. Picture the scene if you can. Excited men, startled women and terrified children trip and tumble in their anxiety to escape the clutches of the Laird, and panting and gasping like brewery horses, they reach the highway.

The Broich follows leisurely. As he walks up the street not even a dog is to be seen, the streets being as deserted as the ruins of Thebes. Doors are barred and blinds are drawn – such is the fear inspired by the appearance of the Laird. Two hours *afterwards the principals and several supporters gather round the Gallows Tree – on the Drummond estate and outside the jurisdiction of Broich – and there preparatory arrangements are made for the fight being fought to the bitter end. But the referee fails to put in appearance. On a search being instituted he is found dead drunk round the corner, with the stakes left in the nearby pub. And so ends the great battle."*

Monzie

Monzie lies to the east of the more populous Parish of Crieff and is that unique place which spans both Highland and Lowland areas. Stobie's map of Perthshire published in 1783, shows the area along the Almond east of the present location of Glenalmond School to have been transferred to Moneydie Parish whilst the wild upland parts above the boulder strewn

OLD ROMAN BRIDGE, MONZIE, NEAR CRIEFF.

The old mill is gone but the "Roman" bridge is still there on the left-hand side of the road after Monzie Kirk.

west side of the Sma' Glen were annexed to Monzie from Fowlis Wester and Crieff Parishes. The first Statistical Account of the parish of Monzie was written by the Rev. George Erskine in the 1790s and he jalouses that the name is derived from the Gaelic, but as to its *"orthography or signification there is some doubt. Some think it should be wrote Monieu which signifies Deer Hill as probably at that period the hills abound with that species of game. Others think it should be wrote Moniui which signifies hill foot and is very expressive of the situation of habitable parts of the Parish. But a third class maintain and with the greatest probability, that it should be wrote Moegbe which signifies good plain, as the low lying grounds are pretty fertile".*

The Second Account written some fifty or so years later has the author (The Rev John Omand) being quite adamant that Monzie is derived from the Gaelic Moighidh meaning a level tract. The name of course is pronounced "Mon-ee" which like Muthill is a name which new comers and tourists find difficult to get correct the first time around. In common with most of the Strath's rural parishes the population shows a drop over the years. In 1755 Dr Webster's head count calculated some 1192 persons which had dropped by a mere 56 persons some 47 years later in the first Statistical Account. When the Second Account was published it revealed that in the head count taken in 1836 the population had fallen to 940 persons or by some 21% overall. During the first half of the 19th century, the focal point of the Parish had moved from the traditional centre, the village of Monzie to the new village of Gilmerton, sitting astride the main Crieff to Perth road and more convenient for access to Crieff with its markets and other facilities. This road had changed from that shown on Stobie's map. The original routing was up the hill and through Fowlis Wester thus avoiding the flood plain of the Earn. No doubt improved drainage and quicker access was why by the second half of the 19th century the present route by the lower ground had become the prime way to Perth and which was to become the A85 trunk road currently in use.

Monzie in the 18th century was described as a Gaelic speaking parish in the back part and with the old Scotch dialect in the fore part, pronounced with the Gaelic tone and accent. *"There are however very few persons in the parish who do not either speak or understand Gaelic."* (First Statistical Account, 1793)

Things however had changed in the next 50 years and we are told that Gaelic is spoken only in *"western Glenalmond whilst elsewhere in the southern districts few even understand the Gaelic, which is sufficient evidence that the ancient tongue is falling into disuse."* (Second Statistical Account, 1843). Today the language of the Garden of Eden has disappeared in entirety.

Chapter 8

The Military Road
of
General Wade

Previously we noted the Roman presence in Strathearn and their control of the area by the construction of forts and watch towers from Ardoch northwards and across the Gask Ridge. Reference to the ordnance survey maps of the area (Pathfinders NN81/91 Auchterarder and Muthill, NN 82/92 Crieff and the smaller scale Landranger Sheet 68 Perth and Kinross) all indicate at various places the lines of "old military roads". The A9 trunk road north of Balhaldie (OS ref NN 813 054) running to Greenloaning is marked with this as is the twisting road between Braco and Comrie know as the "Langside" and the incredibly straight back road between Greenbrae (OS ref 845 119) and Muthill avoiding the wind swept Muir of Orchil. These have probably all got Roman origin connecting camps such as Dalginross in Comrie and the huge base camp at Ardoch.

Road building in Scotland seemed to stagnate for centuries with the Roman departure. Communications between towns and villages utilised the existing and little was done to develop new links. The movement of cattle to the Trysts or markets including of course that at Crieff, saw the emergence of a network of drove roads. These by their very nature tended to avoid villages and small towns and tended to take ways which guaranteed a plentiful supply of fodder en route as the crossed over mountain pass and boggy moor. There had been a vague attempt at remedying the shocking condition of the existing roads when the Scottish Parliament passed an Act in 1669 which introduced an obligation for tenants and cottars to provide labour and where possible a horse and cart for six days per annum in three successive years. Needless to say this was not a success and it was really the deteriorating political climate in Scotland in the 18th century that brought about the transformation. It was an Irishman from County Meath who came from a military background that played a considerable part in the transformation. George Wade was born in 1673. He served in a number of regiments at home and in Europe gaining steady promotion through the ranks. He had been appointed a Brigadier General in 1707 and Major General in 1714. The same year he became MP for a Wiltshire constituency which seemed at that time compatible with an army career. He seems to have arrived in Scotland in 1725 after having successfully put down trouble from West Country Jacobites in Bath. He saw that to control the Highlands a system of roads and forts were essential. After a survey of requirements he applied to the Government for funds for this to be put in hand. Wade the road builder had arrived.

Wade commenced work on the Crieff to Dalnacardoch road. Dalnacardoch lies on the line of the present A9 in Glen Garry north west of Calvine and before the Pass of Drumochter. The new road was to stretch some 44 miles linking up with his road from Dunkeld and stretching northwards to the military barracks at Ruthven, onto Inverness and providing the connection with the Great Glen Forts of Augustus, William and George.

Wade commenced in the then village of Crieff and followed the line of what is now King Street, across James Square and up what was Hill Wynd. The line of Ferntower Road with its Victorian villas follows Wades original road as it enters the policies of what was Ferntower Estate and is now Crieff Golf Course. As the road was primarily for military purposes Wade appears to have chosen the line and carried out the construction without prior consultation with the land owners. When the Campbell Preston family developed the estate on the marriage of Ann Campbell Preston to Sir David Baird in 1810 it is likely that part of the road was obliterated as it passed in front of the mansion house of Ferntower. The well close by was known as Copes Well and is marked on the OS map.

The road turned north before Gilmerton past the entrance to Monzie Castle and runs roughly parallel to the existing A822 main road before crossing over it near the farm known as the Ibert. Much remains of the road and it is still possible to walk much of the original line. An excellent book which covers the history of all of Wades Roads and has copious pictures and maps is *The Wade Roads by Joan and Arthur Baker* (The Melven Press, 1982).

As we move northwards out of Strathearn a number of interesting features deserve comment. In the Sma' Glen (OS ref NN 895 306) lies the great Clach Ossian or Ossian stone. This originally lay in the way of the road builders who with great effort managed to move it out of the way of the proposed line. Beneath the stone was discovered a hollow in which there were ashes and human bone. Contemporary accounts of the time indicate that these were the mortal remains of a Roman officer. The stone lies some two miles north of the Roman camp at Fendoch. A connection would appear highly improbable. The more likely explanation that the remains were much older than this period in our history. The area was occupied by early nomadic farmers as far back as the 4th Millennium BC.

Strathearn has a number of chambered tombs and burial sites attributable to these early inhabitants. Close by (OS ref NN 830 330) on the private road from Newton Bridge to Auchnafree lies Clach na Tiompamn a chambered cairn excavated in 1954 and measuring over two hundred feet in length! The discovery of the bones at the Ossian Stone was followed by the reburial carried out by the local Highland clansman and in Gaelic tradition a volley of gun shot was fired over the new grave. Thereafter speculation grew rife and a report of 1785 by Thomas Newte recounts that he had been informed by the local populous that these had been in fact the remains of a local bard. This coupled by the excitement over MacPherson's "discovery" of Ossian manuscripts at the time seems to have created the legend of the Ossian Stone! Ossian or Oisin Mac Fhinn, the son of Finn or Fingall had been a legendary Celtic poet and warrior who returned from Tir na nog, the land of perpetual youth after a period of 300 years to be converted to Christianity by St Patrick in the 5th century. His connection with the Sma' Glen seems a somewhat specious tale.

Returning to actuality, one finds about a mile onwards just after Newton Bridge a superb little bridge over a tumbling burn. The simple arch and rubble stonework are a tribute to the skill of the workmen of the time. On a different scale from the Wade "master piece" over the Tay at Aberfeldy, this small bridge nevertheless deserves special mention.

We are now well and truly out of the Strath as the road heads for Strathtay by Corrymuckloch, Amulree and the wild moor lands beyond. The road served a purpose to facilitate the movement of troops and thus theoretically help control; the rebellious subjects. In actual fact it enabled quite often the reverse to happen especially with regard to the '45 Uprising as Prince Charlie's men took advantage of the improved access to the south. Apart from the military reasoning behind the Wade roads it undoubtedly proved beneficial in the extreme for many Scots in remoter areas of the country. So perhaps we should recall the oft quoted ditty:

"Had you seen these roads before they were made
You would hold up your hands and bless General Wade."

Chapter 9

THE BURNING OF THE STRATHEARN TOWNS AND VILLAGES

JACOBITE RETALIATION?

Historical background

To properly understand the "burnings", it is necessary to look briefly at the overall history of Scotland prior to the 1715 uprising. The advent of James IV to the throne of Great Britain on the death of Elizabeth of England was significant in a number of ways to every day life in Scotland. James embraced the English Court and the Episcopal form of worship. He introduced what is referred to as The Five Articles, which were pure anathema to the Presbyterians. These were enjoying private baptism, private communion, confirmation by bishops, observance of holy days and kneeling at communion. The General Assembly, the "parliament" of the Kirk rejected these in 1617 but after being passed by the Privy Council, was forced through the following Assembly in 1619. The Scottish Parliament by a small majority gave its sanction to the "Articles". James himself stated "No bishops – no King!" He literally governed by the pen issuing his instructions to the Privy Council. When he died in 1625, his successor was the politically incompetent Charles I. One of his first appointments was Archbishop Spottiswoode as Chancellor. In 1634 the Scottish Parliament presented him with a "supplication" in which their grievances were set out. All to no avail as Charles would not budge on his views. In 1637 he demanded that all Scottish Churches use the new prayer book. The immediate response was the production of the National Covenant in 1638. Its signatories swore to "maintain the form of Church government most in accord with God's will", in other words that of the Presbyterian Kirk. It fomented the Bishop's War (1639/1640) which was led from the front by many of the Nobles such Loudoun and Montrose. The substantial support of the majority of Scottish Lairds was important. "The Wars of the Covenants" brought a whole Nation under arms. They demanded the removal of the Bishops from the Privy Council. This threat of action was sufficient to win their case. The "Three Estates" now saw the Lairds take over from the Bishops and join the Nobles and the representatives of the Burghs and the Shires.

The English Civil War in 1642 saw the supporters of the Covenant throw in their lot with the Parliamentary forces in return for a guarantee of a Presbyterian form of worship not only in Scotland but in England as well (The Solemn League and Covenant). Developments in Scotland saw James Graham, Marquis of Montrose, throw in his lot with the royalists. Although a Presbyterian he wished to safeguard the monarchy. His suspicions had been aroused by the emergence of his arch rival Archibald Campbell, Marquis of Argyll. With the aid of Alasdair Mac Colla or Alasdair MacDonald, Montrose set about his task. Mac Colla was a Highland warrior of rare military talent who was connected with the McDonnels of Antrim. Using this family connection he brought fellow clansmen from Ireland to join up in the struggle.

Montrose waged a successful campaign and won battles at Tibbermore, Kilsyth and Inverlochy before coming a cropper at Philiphaugh. The subsequent defeat of Charles 1 at Naseby saw the collapse of the war. Charles was executed in January 1649. Tibbermore was in particularly apposite to feelings pertaining in Strathearn and was an indication of the split loyalties of the people of the area.

Tibbermore
A bloody encounter

The Battle of Tibbermore was a victory for Montrose. The Government forces under the Earl of Lothian were to march to Perth and Burleigh was to march there from Fife. All able bodied men between 16 and 60 were called to arms in Perthshire (fencibles). Lothian was to drive the rebels north into the arms of Argyll. Montrose with the Stewarts and the Robertsons marched via Aberfeldy and down the Sma' Glen to surprise the opposition. Near Crieff they met a force of 500 Highlanders newly formed by Lord Kilpoint, Sir John Drummond and the Master of Madderty as requested by the regime. All three were obeying orders to join the Covenanters in Perth but had Royalist sympathies. Kilpoint was a Graham, a kinsman of Montrose and Madderty was Montrose's brother in law. It is though that perhaps there was collusion and that was why Montrose came via the Sma' Glen and Crieff. The surprise worked as the Highlanders had a core of Irish veterans under MacColla. Despite being fewer in numbers the ferocity of the charge shattered the Covenanters defence. It turned into a massacre. The Highlanders chased them to Perth and slaughtered all. It is reported (Stevenson, 1980) that one Irish officer stated, *"You could not walk the three miles from the battlefield to Perth without once touching the ground and treading on corpses."* The local Presbyterian minister said, *"The hounds of hell were drawn up before our ports newly bathed in blood and demanding more with hideous cries."*

72

After Tibbermore

There after followed a period of confusion. The Scots supported his son Charles II as legitimate successor on the proviso that he would support the National Covenant and the Solemn League and Covenant. As a result Cromwell invaded Scotland and after a crushing victory at Dunbar quickly took virtual control of the country. Charles was crowned at Scone and Argyll invaded England but was defeated at Worcester. Cromwell was overlord. Both Argyll and his rival Montrose were executed in Edinburgh.

Cromwell died in 1658 and in 1660 Charles II was proclaimed King. Despite the sacrifices that had been made, things quickly reverted to the past. The Recissory Act in 1661 declared all legislation passed since 1633 to be null and void. The Covenants were renounced and Episcopacy restored which meant the hierarchy of Bishops, lay patronage (land owners picked the parish clergy) and royal supremacy with the King as head of the Church. This was the period of the Covenanters, of " conventicles "in Ayrshire and the south west and dissent. Soldiers raised by the Duke of Perth (an Episcopalian) were sent from Strathearn to quell the troubles. They were called the *"Highland Host"*. It was a period known in Scottish history as the *"killing times"*. Ministers of the Kirk circulated papers of dissent against the King. It resulted in Presbyterians being executed for treason.

The Chief official in Scotland was the King's brother James, Duke of York and Albany. He was not an Episcopalian but something even worse in the eyes of many Presbyterians, a convert to Catholicism! In 1685 he succeeded to the throne on Charles's death. In England opposition was strong and William of Orange, ruler of Holland was invited take over the throne. His wife, Mary was James elder daughter.

James went into exile and William became King. Scotland followed suit and when William guaranteed a Presbyterian ascendancy in Church matters he became King of Scotland.

Struggles continued. Claverhouse whom James had created Viscount Dundee moved north and raised an army of James supporters or Jacobites. He moved south and defeated General MacKay at Killiecrankie but was himself shot. The next battle was at Dunkeld where a Cameronian regiment (founded by the original dissenters) held the town against the Jacobites. William demanded Clan chiefs take an oath of allegiance. The Massacre of Glencoe resulted. Feelings in the Highlands were made worse by a number of similar type atrocities. A naval force had attacked Eigg and massacred and violated the people. The matter was hushed up. (Lynch, 1991). The Darien scheme followed authorisation by the Scottish Parliament. It was a disaster and nearly bankrupted the Country. Lack of support from the forces of King William when under attack caused resentment .The Act of Succession was passed by the English Parliament without consultation and the 1705 English Alien Act restricted severely matters of inheritance especially amongst those

Scottish nobles with lands south of the Border. They could not inherit. Such was the turbulent back cloth to the century prior to the first Jacobite Uprising. The 1707 Union of Parliaments had become a fait accompli.

Religious changes locally

To appreciate and understand something of the complexities and attitudes of the times is fundamental to passing judgement on events. Apart from the ever present political intrigue amongst the politically powerful in the land, there had been the religious conflict of the 17th century with the *"killing times"* of the 1680s bringing with it the persecution of the Presbyterians followed abruptly by what has been termed the Revolution of 1688 which brought Protestant William of Orange and his Queen Mary to the throne of the united kingdoms. Here in Strathearn, the problems in the parish church had mirrored the situation in the country at large. The minister was David Drummond an MA of St Andrew's University and a son of James Drummond, the fifth Laird of Milnab. David was from records an astute individual. He had succeeded to the local lands of Kincardine and Trytoun and had purchased the lands of Callander near Barvick and with it the benefits of the teinds (a form of rent) which supplemented his stipend. Although Drummond had supported the National Covenant in 1638 with its declaration of Presbyterian convictions and resistance to Episcopacy, he had supported the Royalist cause during the Civil War for which he was deposed from his ministry by the General Assembly of the Kirk. In fact their powers were such that Drummond continued to administer to his flock in Crieff as well as draw his stipend before eventually relinquishing his charge in 1658.

The local conflict was to continue with the appointment of Gilbert Murray as successor to Drummond. Like Drummond, Murray was from the same background as Drummond being related to the Murrays of Ochtertyre. He was immediately in conflict with the Presbytery when it was averred that he was in collusion with his predecessor Drummond and that the two were in fact sharing the stipend between them! Murray refused to appear to be questioned about *"the scandalous action"* and seemed to spend more time adapting his religious affiliations to the mood of the day. From being initially a staunch Presbyterian he became an Episcopalian but was allowed to continue his ministry! His son William succeeded him in 1682 and quickly nailed his colours to the mast and made no bones the fact that he too was a convinced Episcopalian. No doubt to rub salt into the wounds of the Presbytery he introduced forms of worship which were an anathema to the traditional kirk. The Lord's Prayer was used in worship, the Apostles' Creed was repeated at baptisms and the Doxology was sung by the congregation.

Whether or not the somewhat independent views of the ministers in Crieff during the turbulent years of the 17th century indicated a degree of local support we shall probably never know. It is clear that the participating congregation as they worshipped in the old kirk in what is now Church Street were indeed participants in the acts of worship be they "*Piscy*" or not! With the succession of William and Mary in 1688, things however changed. Murray was deposed from his ministry for reading part of Psalm 118 after the Jacobite victory at Killiecrankie: "*This is the day God made, in it we'll joy triumphantly!*" In 1690 Episcopacy was overthrown and the Presbyterian form of worship was formally re introduced with the Westminster Confession adopted as the Confession of the Church. For a period of 9 years the turbulent charge of the Crieff Parish Church lay vacant until in 1699 when along came yet another Drummond!

John Drummond unlike his immediate predecessors had been educated at Glasgow University. His was a conformity to the established kirk and despite a flirtation with what was to become the first of the Secessionist groups (this caused him to be disciplined by the Presbytery), he stayed in charge in Crieff for some 55 years including the period of the first Jacobite uprising. It was John Drummond who wrote the account of the burning of Crieff. His and local Church attitudes towards the Stewart dynasty can be discerned from the records of the time. Minutes refer to a "*horrid abuse committed by some persons in the town of Crieff, by their drinking King James' health publicly at the Cross and abusing several inhabitants in the town.*" Mr Drummond was requested to draw up a list of offenders for the attention of the Queen's Advocate. The regenerated kirk was determined to exert its authority on one and all. A Session minute is indicative of strict discipline they wished to exert on the local populous particularly in relation to the Sabbath. It notes "*the frequent profanation of the Lord's Day by unnecessary walking in the fields, idle talking, bearing of water, taking in of kail and the like.*" Elders were asked to "*take strict notice*" of such infringements, with a view to discipline.

This was the atmosphere that prevailed in this part of Strathearn. During the most part of the 17th century there was clearly a strong local support for the Episcopalian attitude and ipso facto the Jacobite cause. This was no doubt affected somewhat by the "glorious revolution" of 1688 and the subsequent clamp downs on attitude and civic discipline by the sentinels of a more Calvinistic kirk both locally and further afield in Strathearn.

The 1714 Uprising

Sheriffmuir was fought on the 13th of November 1715. The Jacobite army was led by the Earl of Mar and the Hanoverians by the Duke of Argyll. The Highlanders held Perth and moved onto Auchterarder where the army was assembled. It was nearly 9,000 strong and was more or less all of Highland composition. Argyll was based in Stirling and marched out on the 12 of November. His army was just over 3,000 in strength and comprised English soldiers and groups such as the Glasgow Volunteer Regiment and the

Stirling County Militia. They moved onto the high ground above Dunblane. The Jacobites moved out of Kinbuck and took the high ground near what is now Whitestone Rifle Range. The battle was hesitant and indecisive. Marr was over cautious. Both armies retreated. The Government troops had losses of 663 men, the Jacobites 232. Although a nominal victory for the Jacobites it was the beginning of the end. He retreated, troops deserted and he embarked on the scorched earth policy of destroying the towns and villages between him and Argyll, namely Crieff, Auchterarder, Dunning, Muthill, Blackford and Dalreoch. The accounts were all written by the Presbyterian Ministers of the various places. These were later collated by the Maitland Club in the 1840s and published. They were transcribed and reprinted in various books of the times such as Porteous and the Annals of Auchterarder. What is not generally reported is the original preface. The Chairman of the Club at that time was the incumbent Duke of Argyll whose ancestor led the Government forces at Sheriffmuir. This in itself reflects in the academic and historical nature of the reporting. The passage of time, some one hundred and twenty five years, since the event ensures that it is a record of the reporting of the day. The preface, which has been greatly ignored in previous accounts, emphasised the reasoning behind the burnings, the scorched earth policy and the dire need of the Jacobites to prevent supplies in the depth of a cruel winter falling into Hanoverian hands. It particularly draws attention to the bias of the contemporary reporters namely that of the local Presbyterian ministers.

Preface to the Burning Reports Published by The Maitland Club

NB The following was copied in 1995 from the transcriptions of the above mentioned Club from documents held in the Mitchell Library in Glasgow.

"The following documents relate to a period near the end of the Civil War of 1715/16 when the hopes of the Jacobite Army under the Earl of Mar at Perth and attended by the Chevalier in person (then recently arrived in Scotland) were limited to making a successful stand for a little time within or in front of that town against the superior forces of the Duke of Argyll who was expected immediately to march against them from Stirling for the purpose of putting an end to the insurrection. The county was covered with deep snow and it was thought necessary by the Jacobite chiefs to add to the difficulties of the Duke's intended march by burning all the villages destroying as far as possible the grain and other provisions lying between Stirling and Perth. This severe measure was executed by detachment of the Clans and produced of course great misery to the people of the devastated district. These Duncrub papers, the composition apparently of a person friendly to the Government but probably faithful with regard to the facts give minute accounts of the various transactions.

It has been thought proper since the tone of the narratives is so unfavourable to the insurgent party to add for the sake of impartiality a letter addressed by the Chevalier when about to embark at Montrose, to the Duke of Argyll in which not only does the writer express the regret of a benevolent mind for an act which the necessities of war alone could justify but states that he had taken measures to repair as far as he could, the evils there by inflicted on so many innocent persons.

After all hopes of executing the will of the Chevalier had been abandoned by General Gordon and that they were carried abroad in The letter appears to have been left with the commander of the remnant of the insurgent army along with an order empowering him to forward it to the Duke of Argyll and at the same time to deposit a sum of money for the compensation of the sufferers in the hands of the magistrates of some town as might be convenient at the time.

Probably neither was the letter delivered nor the money paid but the fact of the effort by the Chevalier offers a satisfactory view of a character which every successive publication of exerts from the Stuart papers has made the more and more amiable and respectable.

The letter and order have been preserved in the family of Sir Peter Murray Threipland of Fingask, baronet, and a circumstance which makes it probable that the design of the Chevalier was never executed. The ancestor of this gentleman, Sir David Threipland was one of the persons in arms and he contrived with one or two others to get to France in a vessel from the Moray Firth.It seems probable that the letter and order had come into Sir David's hands the first place and afterwards preserved merely as memorabilia by the head of the House of Stuart."

Copied from the Maitland Club Papers in the Mitchell Library Glasgow, 1995.

What really happened?

What actually happened then in the run up and in the aftermath of Sheriffmuir? James VIII had as his Chief of Staff the Earl of Mar who had originally sworn loyalty to George I but had been snubbed by the monarch thus causing him to switch allegiance to the Stewart cause and the Old Pretender. Mar has been described as many things by many people but it is clear that when he returned somewhat surreptitiously to Scotland from the Hanoverian Court in London after yet a second rebuttal from George. His pique no doubt rekindled and inflamed his enthusiasm for James for he set about recruiting influential people to the Jacobite cause as soon as he landed in Fife. The story of the 1714 is long and complex and outwith the scope of this book. Let it suffice to say that immediately prior to the Battle of Sheriffmuir on Sunday the 13th of November 1715, Mar was billeted at Perth and his rival Argyll at Dunblane. Strathearn stretched out between them. Auchterarder featured as a staging post for Mar. A week earlier the western clans, approximately 2,500 strong arrived in the town. These comprised the MacDonalds of Sleat, MacDonalds of Clanranald, MacDonald of Glencoe, MacDonald of Glengarry, the MacDougalls, the MacLeans, the Camerons of Lochiel and the Stuarts of Appin. The army was reviewed on Auchterarder Moor. It now numbered some 8,797 men including Rob Roy and his

Macgregors. The battle was a bit of a non-event or in modern parlance, hand bags at fifty paces! Mar proved indecisive and failed to exert his numerical superiority. Argyll and the Hanoverians who numbered a mere 3,210 men were let off the hook. Casualties showed Argyll to have lost nearly 700 men whilst the Jacobites lost a mere 232.

What followed thereafter is the real subject of this tale. Mar had retreated to Perth. Argyll had sent out a scouting party of his dragoons from Dunblane and accompanied them himself. Their main intention was to appraise the road system and in doing so they reached as far as Auchterarder. Exaggerated reports of the strength of the party reached Perth. It was thought that some 3,000 men were moving forward and an attack was imminent. The scorched earth policy was put into action to prevent Argyll getting his hands on supplies. The weather at the time (January 1716) was fiendish. There was thick snow, then a rapid thaw and another heavy fall of snow.

The burnings were carried out by Clan Ranald whose brother had been killed at Sheriffmuir. His 600 Camerons and MacDonalds fired first Auchterarder, then Blackford and then Crieff. The Crieff conflagration was assisted by Ludovic Drummond who was factor to Lord Drummond who it was alleged was delighted to take revenge on those who had failed to support the Jacobite cause. The feelings were high and it took a long time for compensation to be paid to the unfortunate citizens of the towns and villages destroyed. The minister's report praised one Jacobite, one of the local Lairds namely Anthony Murray of Dollerie whose family still reside to the east of Crieff. Murray had implored with compatriots to desist from their orders and save the town. It was to no avail. The Rev Drummond's account is indeed graphic and obviously was seen by him as the inevitability of being persecuted by "*wicked men compassing their designs of settling a Popish pretender upon the Throne.*"

In conclusion hindsight perhaps draws the conclusion that the whole episode was unnecessary. Mar fluffed his chances at Sheriffmuir and authorised what was really a needless destruction of the towns and villages. Notwithstanding the recorded writings of the Calvanistic ministers with their deep seated hatred of "papists and their like", it was clear that Strathearn was a divided community and not simply a split between Highlander and Lowlander, Episcopalian and Presbyterian, Catholic and Protestant.

The sadness is that geography had placed the Strath in the cockpit of a potentially National conflict between diametrically opposed factions. It stood in the way of the opposing forces and as such it was inevitable in the circumstances the one or other of the parties would employ a scorched earth policy. Historical accuracy and not biased sectarianism should be the accountant.

Jacobite influence in Strathearn

To date, the accounts of the *"Burnings"* have, as related above been based on the accounts of the local Presbyterian clergy incumbent at the time. The Kirk of course was at that time beginning to fragment into various seceding groups, all at each others throat over some seemingly relevant matter of Presbyterian government. Despite the various factions, burgher or anti burgher, auld licht or new licht, they were all violently opposed to the recently overthrown Episcopalianism or, say it quietly, the Papists of the *"auld faith"*! Respected historians such as Reid in his *Annals of Auchterarder* and Porteous in his *History of Crieff* both reported but did not analyse the background to the *"burnings"*. What is perhaps not appreciated in this present age is that prior to both Uprisings, Strathearn was firmly owned and managed by the Jacobite faction. Fortunately we have a detailed list of names, places, rent rolls, stock and crops from the information collated by the Commissioners of Forfeited Estates and published by the Scottish Record Office in 1973. In the interests of historical impartiality the following is an abstract of the Earl of Perth's confiscated holdings in 1755.

1. **Barony of Lix (NB the lands above Glen Ogle, north of Lochearnhead):** 4 farms, 28 families, 128 persons.

2. **Barony of Balquhidder:** 8 farms, 68 families, 257 persons.

3. **Barony of Comrie:** 21 farms, 182 families, 777 persons.

4. **Un named Barony including Findoglen, Achnashellach and the Culnacarries:** 4 farms, 21 families and 99 persons.

5. **Parish of Muthill:** 88 farms or possessors, 391 families, 1639 persons.

6. **Barony of Auchterarder:** 32 farms or possessors, 62 families, 261 persons.

7. **Barony of Kinbuck:** 7 farms, 33 families, 194 persons.

8. **Barony of Callendar:** 32 farms or possessors, 123 families, 523 persons.

9. **Barony of Strath Gartney:** 14 farms, 100 families, 414 persons.

10. **Barony of Milnab and the Town of Crieff:** 52 farms or possessors, 207 families, 778 persons.

11. **Barony of Stobhall (un life rented):** 3 farms , 31 families, 132 persons.

12. **Barony of Stobhall (life rented):** 27 farms, 208 families, 990 persons.

What does the above prove? In Highland, and indeed Scottish society of the time the tenants enjoyed the support and protection of the Laird or Clan chief. The Earls of Perth or the Drummond family could call upon from the above in excess of 6,000 individuals or well in excess of 50% of the population. It is clear that whilst not everyone amongst his tenants would raise sword, a great many, such as the Drummonds of Trian in Glen Artney would and did for a cause that their Chief believed to be just.

In the course of my researching the "burnings" and the conflicting evidence, I unearthed an interesting little piece recounted by that eminent historian and antiquarian RS Fittes whose incredible works are safely ensconced in the AK Bell Library in Perth as part of the Sandeman Collection and readily available for future historians to peruse and formulate their own opinions. There is a collection of Perthshire Ballads, Rhymes and Fragments collected and recounted by one T (Omar) M, the pseudonym for the Rev. Thomas Morris who died at the tragically young age of 30 years in 1870s. The Rev. Tom was by all accounts a goodly man. His epitaph recalls his valiant work amongst the poor of Edinburgh. He was by all accounts a chirpy, cheerful person who in his short life span brought a fine degree of Christian charity to the underprivileged of *"Auld Reekie"*. He can have had little or any personal experience of Perthshire and its people, yet he is vehement in his condemnation of Jacobites and assumes without stated proof that the populace of the County were violently opposed to the Stewarts and all they stood for in politics and religion. His works include the following piece of poetry headed:

Anti-Jacobite Fragments

Saw ye Eppie Marley, honey
The woman that sells the barley, honey ?

She's lost her pocket and a' her money,
Wi following Jacobite Charlie, honey.

Eppie Marley's turned sae fine,
She'll no gang out to herd the swine,
but lies in her bed till eight or nine,
And winna come down the stairs to dine.

LI

The king o' France he ran a race,
Out ower the hills o' Styria
His auldest son did follow him,

Upon a good grey meerie-a.

And they rade east , and they rade west ,
And they rade far and neerie-a;
Until they came to Sherramuir,
When they dang them tapsel-teerie-a.

The cat has kittled in Charlie's wig,

The cat has kittled in Charlie's wig,
There's ane o' them living, and twa o' them dead;

The cat has kittled in Charlie's wig.

"The last time Perthshire was in the depths of a severe political contest, a historical blunder was perpetrated, we know not by which side, and repeated with with little or no variation by the entire press of the country – south of the Tweed not less than in the north. This blunder consisted in attributing a political victory to the deep-rooted veneration in the popular mind for the historical name of Charles Stewart, – the young Pretender.

No mistake could be more complete, especially in regard to Perthshire, as Jacobite documents now before the World clearly shows. 'Notwithstanding my endeavours to raise men in an amicable way, yet I find will be impossible to accomplish it without a party', wrote one. 'For God's sake, send up our recruits' – wrote another. 'I find the backwardness of the men's rising is much, if not altogether, owing to the irresoluteness of the gentleman,' wrote a third Jacobite leader in the County in the progress of the rising in 1745; while the comic old veteran, Robertson of Strowan, addressed the Duke that he was apprehending all deserters who came his way, and was 'sorry to see that all are Running to the Devil but the Duke of Atholl and the L—d of Str–n.'

If the people of Scotland ever were Jacobites, it must have been, – after the fact. Any popular sympathy which ever existed for the unfortunate Stewarts, can claim no higher name than compassion for the sufferers from misfortune; and it is attributable mainly, if not exclusively, to the splendid minstreley which succeeded the House of Stewart. Scotland as a nation never participated, except to support the House of Hanover, in the risings of 1715 and 1745; which is easily accounted for by the intense Presbyterianism of the Scottish people, and the Prelacy of the Rebels."

The Rev. Tom was a good man but seemed as sadly to be a typical Presbyterian of his time with an inbred aversion for those who professed their Christianity in another form. His outspeakings and historical pronouncements seem totally devoid of source or indeed fact. It is doubtful whether he ever set foot in Strathearn but nevertheless felt competent to pass judgement on the attitude and opinions of its citizens. Indeed one wonders whether he had ever heard of or indeed knew of his Presbyterian associates in Crieff. If he had, perhaps his outpourings may have been less vociferous. I do not presume for one minute that he had ever heard of Gilbert Murray, Minister of Crieff in 1680, who started off as a staunch Presbyterian but became an Episcopalian yet continued to administer to his flock in Crieff or indeed his son William who on succeeding him introduced into the worship in Strathearn, the Lords Prayer, the Doxology and the

Apostles' Creed all of which were anathema to the Presbyterians of the Lowlands! In addition to that we have of course the Minister of Crieff Kirk who read the 118th Psalm after the Jacobite victory at Killiekrankie joyously pronouncing to his congregation that "This is the day God made, in it We'll joy triumphantly". The Jacobite leanings of the local Kirk and most probably it's congregation were under pressure in the early 1700s when the then Minister, John Drummond was asked by the Presbytery to draw up a list of offenders (for the attention of the Queen's Advocate) who had *"committed a horrid abuse by drinking King James' health publically at the Cross."*

Needless to say the outcome was zilch! No doubt if he ever became aware of this unseemly Presbyterian behaviour, the good Tom will still be birling in his grave!

To appreciate the strong religious influence on the people of post '45 Scotland, one has only to refer back to the printed word of the day. The broad sheets were not governed to the same extent as their modern counterparts. The professed view in many cases depicted not that of the paper's readers but that of the proprietors or indeed the Kirk Session. The following was reported in a contemporary periodical of the day {The Perth Constitutional}. *"The Perth UP Presbytery must have been a patriotic body during the Rebellion. Speaking at Mr Paton's ordination dinner, the Clerk of the Presbytery {Rev JC Inglis, Crieff} stated that when looking over some old minutes, he came across the following curious entry: It was reported at a meeting of the Presbytery of Perth, that last night a public enemy, in Prince Charles Stuart, had seized the City of Perth, and the members there and then agreed to go back to their congregations and pray loyally for King George. I record the above incident for the benefit of future historians of the ecclesiastical history of Perth."* The Rev John C Ingles (sic) was minister in Crieff between 1870 and 1910 of what was St Andrew's Church in Strathearn Terrace and which after amalgamation with the Parish Kirk of St Michael's across the road became the "church hall" of the united body. Ingles was somewhat unique in that Crieff North United Presbyterian Congregation was his sole administration in some forty years of steward-ship. I am not certain whether Mr Ingles believed or not in his seceder roots but what he pronounced showed yet again that Presbyterians in the post Charlie era were still in a Tibbermore trauma!

Evaluation

In evaluating historical topics, one can generally adopt one of two strategies. The first is *"hypothesis testing"* where one examines and explores the evidence based on specific evidence available. The second is a *"questioning sources"* strategy where interpretation of a variety of sources leads to arriving at an opinion based on a balanced judgement. I have attempted to look at the *"burnings"* in a broader context than that presented in the past. As a card carrying member of the *"Kirk"* and an impartial historian, I am conscious that the written record, has until recently, not been truly objective. I trust the above perhaps redresses the balance.

Chapter 10

Witchcraft in Strathearn

Some strange tales

It was not just in Salem that witches were reputed to exist and suffered the ultimate punishment in the hunts that followed. In Strathearn the number of persons persecuted for allegedly practising the black art was not inconsiderable. Before looking at the various stories that were recorded then and thereafter, it is appropriate that we look at the historical background. Prior to the Reformation there existed a somewhat ambivalent attitude to witches, warlocks and sorcerers. Indeed the prosecutions for witchcraft in Scotland were minimal (Smout TC, A History of the Scottish People, Collins, 1972). Between the years 1560 to 1707 however more than 3 000 and possibly up to 4500 were killed in a barbaric retribution for their *"sins"*. Why did this occur in Scotland whilst in England similar punishments tallied about 1000? Superstitious, mediaeval Scotland was thick into the worship of saints and the dark world of the supernatural was accepted as was their customs. If you did not know you did not tamper.

The Reformation brought about a change in attitude highlighted by Calvin's philosophy that the Bible teaches that there are witches and that they must be slain. James VI published in 1597 his treatise Daemonoligie. Knox himself supported the literal text that *"thou shall not suffer a witch to live"*. We now entered a terrifying period when persons accused of witchcraft were tried and disposed of in a truly barbaric fashion. After 1563 Parliament decreed death for anyone practising witchcraft or consulting a witch.

It was in this environment that Perthshire and indeed Strathearn came to the fore in the hunt to find and punish those involved in witchcraft. In Scotland in 1662 some 150 persons were executed. Reid in his *Annals of Auchterarder* recounts that Alexander Colville, His Majesty's Justice Depute for Scotland presided over five trials in the Parish of Fossoway in the ancient Stewartry of Strathearn. These took place in the Crook of Devon. Thirteen persons were accused of forming a coven and one, Robert Wilson was described as a warlock with twelve accomplices as his *"deal's dozen"* and described as witches. One Christian Grieve was put to trial in July, 1662 and found not guilty.

Some three months later the poor woman was brought again in front of the same jury and judge, found guilty without any additional evidence, duly convicted, strangled and burnt five days after. The Court sat in Crook of Devon on a regular basis, as often as five times in all in 1662. The juries were according to Reid, *"formed of men of position"*. The prosecutions were got up by the Laird of Tullibole assisted by his Baillie and the ministers of Fossoway, Kinross, Cleish and Muckhart. It was these individuals who were instrumental in exhorting confessions and admissions from the accused. In all cases the judgement was strangulation followed by burning. This must go down as perhaps one the most cruel and barbaric periods in the Straths' history.

We have still to this day, a reminder of that evil and indeed sad period in our local history. If you take the back road from Glen Devon to Dunning you see on the left hand side of the road about a mile short of the village, a rough stone cairn with the hand painted sign saying it was erected to the memory of Maggie Wall burnt as a witch. Appropriately the cairn is surmounted by a simple cross. The monument is kept in regular repair by persons unknown and is a late tribute to someone who suffered at the hands of the zealots of the time.

The practise of witchcraft or indeed the alleged practising seems from the paucity of available records to have been centred mainly around the Glendevon parish. Porteous in his History of Crieff recounts that in 1692 the Presbytery signed a petition to the Privy Council in regard to a charge of witchcraft against one Alexander Drummond indweller in Auchterarder. The petition bore that Drummond *"hes these many yeris ago bein ane most notorious abuser of God's peopill in many places of this kingdome by charmes, inchantments and other divellish and unlawfull meanes, and by the gritt concurse of all sorts of peopill, quho upon the report of his fame (quhilk hes lasted nor fyftie yeirs) did resort to him from all the quarters of this realme, did sett up ane publict seatt of abuse in dispyt both of Kirk and cuntrey, quhairby he has involved not only a gritt many ignorants , quho yit attend his oracles and bewitching consenages, bot also many gud Christians in a most dangerous guylyines, undwer collour of giving them the bodily health, quhilk he pretends to doebe lawfull and physicall meanes, quhairof he is altogidder ignorant, as salbe weifified be the dispositioun of many famous witnesses quho have alreddy declared that his cures ar all magicall, fearfully uncouth and unlaufull."*

Drummond had already been denounced twice in Court and was presently a prisoner in Stirling. Not satisfied that he was really in safe custody the *"sapient ministers"* now petitioned that he be *"transported to Edinburgh and keiped in sure firmance, thair to be tryed be his Majesties Justice and Advocat that god may gitt glory and his Kirk on Earth may be purged of sic a pestiferous and scandalous instrument"*.

Drummond was duly tried in Edinburgh, found guilty and burned at the Mercat Cross.

Kate McNiven in Monzie near Crieff was condemned as a witch and was publicly burned on the Knock of Crieff. Her tale is well remembered and oft repeated in this part of the Strath and indeed there are still persons of that name living in the vicinity. The cliff upon which the poor lass met her final fate is still marked on the Ordnance Survey sheet as Kate McNiven's Crag. What then was the nature of the crime for which she was accused of and condemned those centuries ago? Kate worked for one of the landed families of the area namely the Grahams of Inchbrakie, a cadet branch of that mighty Clan whose titular head was the famous Marquis of Montrose. Kate walked each day the 2 or 3 miles from the village of Monzie to the mansion of Inchbrakie now no longer standing having being been sadly demolished in the earlier part of the 20th century. The young nursemaid was blamed for the regular bouts of sickness of her charge, young Master Graham. Eventually Inchbrakie sacked her to the relief of the other servants. From that moment onwards a succession of weird happenings began to occur most being attributed to the malevolent nature of the recently departed Kate.

One day in the course of business, the laird travelled across the Strath a short journey to the picturesque village of Dunning, which coincidentally was another Graham stronghold. In those days it was the custom to take with you on the trip your own cutlery. During the meal, he could not get peace for a bumble bee buzzing around him. In exasperation, he managed to get hold of it and liberate out of one of the windows. When he returned to the table he discovered to his astonishment that his knife and fork had vanished! Together with the servants he searched high and low but to no avail. They had truly vanished! To his utter surprise, when he returned to Inchbrakie the missing implements were there in their usual place. This together with a succession of other inexplicable events galvanised action from the authorities. Kate was brought to court, tried and convicted of witchcraft. The fate was strangulation and burning. Her former employer pleaded for the sentence to be commuted but to no avail. She was dragged up the northeast face of the Knock to the steep cliff where such sentences were carried out. She was tied to the stake and the faggots piled round her. Inchbrakie had just arrived to plead vainly for clemency. Kate spotted him in the crowd and called for him to come towards her. As he did this, she lowered her head and bit off a blue bead from her necklace and spat the stone at him. As he bent to pick it up she shouted that she was grateful for his attempts to obtain her release and that she was giving him this as a keepsake. Kate however declared loudly to the gathered assembly that as long as the family kept the stone in Inchbrakie House itself, their line would never die out.

The stone was set in a golden ring and kept in accordance with Kate's instructions. It was kept in a casket and only daughter in laws were permitted to touch it. Many years later in the mid 1800s it is recorded that, when most of the family were abroad, the then head one Patrick Graham opened a box of papers which had been left in his care only to find amongst them the stone set in the ring, but no longer protected within the walls of Inchbrakie. Within a few years, some ground was sold. Now, the Graeme's of Inchbrakie no longer reside there. Their ancient home has long since been flattened. The lands now lie within those of the Drummond Morays of Abercairney. Traces of the gardens exist and the house called Belle Vue built about ten years ago (c 1990) replaced the cottages occupied by the of the staff of the old house. There is however a pleasing addendum to this tale . I had mentioned this tale whilst talking to the local "Thirty Club" in the Drummond Arms, Crieff. Local farmer, Andrew Comrie, informed me that there was a memorial to the Graeme's within the grounds of the former estate. As a follow up, I spoke to Grace Cuthbert (née McOmish) who had been brought up in Inchbrakie Lodge. Grace not only provided me with a picture of the memorial but also lent me an etching of the majestic Inchbrakie House in its hay day in the 18th century prior to its sad demise (see attached page 124). The small mausoleum like structure was built by the scions of the Inchbrakie family from stones salvaged from the demolished mansion on the original site which is still in possession of the Graeme family. The family now reside in Devon far from their ancestral roots. The current head of this noble branch of the Graham Clan, Mr Anthony Graeme of Inchbrakie still visits Strathearn on a regular basis to ensure that this symbolic reminder of by gone days is properly maintained, a small but important part of Strathearn's heritage.

The general feeling amongst the ecclesiastics of the Reformed church in Strathearn during this period was a venomous hatred of those who dared differ from their narrow viewpoint. Their obsession with finding witches under every bed seemed particularly Scottish although strangely enough replicated in the New World with the Salem Witch trials of 1692. In Salem today witches are big business with the tourists flocking in to Massachusetts to find out the stories of the past. The parallel between Salem and Glendevon is uncannily similar. In both cases the victims were most often women whose behaviour or economic circumstances were somehow disturbing to the social order and conventions of the time. Some of the accused had previous records of criminal activity including witchcraft, but others were faithful churchgoers and people of standing in the community. Although these names have largely been forgotten and indeed the very happenings carefully expurgated from our historical memories, it would be pleasing that at some future date Strathearn acknowledged the past and some fitting record of those sad days is recorded for visitor and local alike.

Strange happenings

City Prices – The Shop in Church Street

Over the years a variety of tales have been told of some strange happenings in a number of places in the Strath. Not all are dredged from ancient memory! Indeed a number of incidents have made the pages of the both the *Strathearn Herald* and the *Courier*. In most cases these have been experienced by different people on different occasions. In 1999, these papers ran accounts of strange happenings in that *"Aladdin's Cave"* of a shop, known as City Prices in Church Street. According to the proprietor John Randles there had been a number of *"happenings"* which could not be logically explained. I have known John for many years and found him to be a straight forward, no nonsense Glaswegian. He is certainly not one to make up such tales for some cheap publicity. What happened was a series of moving objects, feelings of an unnatural presence and when John was alone a loud series of coughs. His partner Liz Cramb has heard the heavy front door open noisily only to find it locked tightly shut when investigated. Local researcher David Cowan has published works on ley lines emanating from the many standing stones in the area. His theory is that the locus of John's shop is really the reason. According to Cowan a powerful ley line runs through the shop plus the fact that adjoining it is Crieff's ancient burial ground. This was "landscaped" a few years back and many stones were disturbed or removed in the process. These factors as well as the presence of an underground watercourse below the shop are, according to him, the probable reasons for these strange happenings. To emphasise that this was no new phenomenon, the press coverage elicited a letter from an Allan Graeme Ramsey whose father Graeme Ramsay ran the shop as an ironmongers in the 1950s. *"My sister Fiona, clearly remembers playing in the rear of the shop after school while my mum helped my dad in the front, and telling them afterwards that she was playing with the other 'lady'. My sister remembers seeing another lady on numerous occasions but I guess my mum and dad thought it was only the vivid imagination of a young child. It was only when we were older that dad talked of the ghost that visited the back shop."*

The Witch of Pittentian

I enjoy the stroll along the path beyond the old farm of Kincardine heading eastwards towards Crieffvechter and above Pittentian. It was here that a number of persons have encountered the witch of Pittentian! On one occasion a mother with her four children was out for a stroll when, to their astonishment, they sighted an old grey haired women coming towards them. What caused the excitement was the fact that below her green cape and hood she seemed to have no visible means of support – her legs were missing! The little group halted in shock as the apparition came closer and closer. Just as she reached the spot where they had halted, the old woman whirled round and disappeared from sight! This apparition has appeared to more than a few Crieff folk. There seems no logical explanation. History fails to offer a tale to conjure with! I have heard that the name Pittentian is derived from the old Pictish and means *"the place of the witch"*. I have also been told that the appearance of the old hag has occurred whilst tests have been carried out in and around not too distant standing stones into the energy or ley lines. But that sounds like yet another story!

An Interesting Discovery Near Crieff

In 1893, it was reported in the local press that a party of workmen working on a new putting green for the extension to the private Dornoch golf course came upon a skeleton of a full grown man about two feet below the surface. This part of the course was known locally as the "*Fairy Knowe*". Round and about 25 yards in diameter at the base, it rises to about 20' to an apex of 4 yards in diameter where the skeleton was found. To all appearances, the body had been deposited with great care, the head lying due east, protected with two boulders, which were placed on each side. The skeleton was very decomposed but its teeth were remarkably well preserved. The mound was within a short distance of the Highlandman Station and could be easily spotted from the railway carriage windows in passing.

For generations, the inhabitants of Crieff and District have associated the Knowe with fairy lore, and the following tradition connected with it may prove interesting.

In olden times, when broguers and shoemakers regularly attended country markets, the story goes that two worthies belonging to the gentle craft from the neighbourhood of Auchterarder, were at the Crieff Michaelmas Market, their goods being carried in satchels which were hung over their shoulders. When the day's marketing was over there was a quantity of their goods unsold. After partaking of some refreshment they slung their satchels over their shoulders and proceeded on their homeward march by the road leading past Dalpatrick to the ford on the Earn. When passing the Fairy Knowe it was well in the night, and on looking in that direction they saw the fairies in their hall within the Knowes holding high carnival – it being their annual festival. The two shoemakers gazed for a while on the scene, and felt themselves involuntarily drawn towards the Knowe. The music, scenery and dancing put them into ecstasies, and one of them was constrained to join in the festivities, and he was instantly whirled round and round in paroxysms of delight, his satchel swinging with him. His friend managed to keep outside and tried by signs and sounds to while his neighbour from the fairies, but nothing would avail. In a short time the scene was changed, the Knowe was closed and the broguer outside had to toddle home much depressed.

Next year, at the same time, he again attended Michaelmas Market and knowing the annual festival of the fairies would take place that night, and it would be the only chance he would have for a twelve months to free his cronie, he resolved to have his marketing done in time to be at the Knowe before midnight. In due time he arrived at the spot and as soon as the performances commenced he descried his companion as he left him the previous year, dancing and capering prodigiously. The broguer outside pulled his bonnet firmly over his brow and rushing amongst the fairies seized his crony and pushed him out of the enchanted circle, and he was immediately brought back to his senses. He put his hand to his shoulder and easing his satchel remarked that it felt unusually heavy. It was believed that he had been dancing continuously during his fascinating captivity and was unconscious of fleeting time. The weight of the brogues in his satchel had made his shoulder feel tired during his year's dance.

Mr John Dron, the farmer at Dornock, after Tuesday's find, caused further excavations of the mound to be made, with the result that more remains were discovered yesterday. The most important is a cist or stone coffin, measuring 3.5 x 2.5 feet. Four stones were laid on edge; underneath in which was an urn full of dark sandy – looking dust, apparently burn matter. Around and below the cist were a number of skeletons, the bones being much decayed. All the skeletons had small boulders at each side of the head, and lay east and west, the head being on the west side.

Chapter 11

Strathearns Highland Heritage

As we have noted elsewhere, Strathearn lies at the gateway to the Highlands or indeed the converse! We know from the detailed Statistical Accounts prepared initially at the end of the 18th century that many of the parishes of Strathearn like Comrie, Monzievaird, Monzie and Fowlis Wester actually were split into two distinct parts, one where Gaelic was the language of all and the other where the inhabitants conversed in Scots in the Lowland fashion. The tales of our Highland heritage concern mainly that part of the Strath to the west where the majestic peaks of Ben Vorlich, Ben More and Ben Ledi dominate. The area around Loch Earn and nearby Balquhidder home of the McGregors.

The Neishes and McNabs

Just out from the delightful village of St Fillans at the eastern end of Loch Earn lies a small island called Neish Island or the Isle of Morell. Like many islands of this size in western Perthshire it is somewhat different from the norm. The island is in fact a crannog or man made island. These were constructed by early man around 2000 BC and examples have been found not only in Loch Earn but also in nearby Loch Tay to the north. Indeed a visit to Kenmore at the east end of Loch Tay will bring you to a superb recreation near the outdoor centre at Crof na caber. The crannog was constructed near the shore with timbers driven into the loch bed in the style of piles in modern construction . The timber platform provides an area for both people and animals whilst the drawbridge link with the shore could be drawn up to protect the crannog dwellers from attack either by animals or indeed from human marauders.

Neish Island was the home of the chieftain of the Neishes, a sept of the Clan McGregor who lived around this part of Strathearn and nearby Balquhidder. Across the hills in the area where Killin now is, dwelt the Clan McNab. Rivalry between the two neighbours was legendary and many a skirmish occurred between the two clans. One particularly bloody incident happened in the early part of the 16th century when the fighting became so intense that it was reported that both sets of combatants disrobed themselves of the encumbrances of their traditional plaids and fought it out clad only in their rough footwear! In this instance the McNabs were triumphant and only twenty McNeishes survived.

In the Highlands memories linger on and nearly one hundred years later a few McNabs were returning from the market town of Crieff laden with Christmas fair when they were waylaid by a band of Neishes who relieved them of their provisions. Surprisingly enough they let them go to return to Killin. The Neishes happened to own the only boat on Loch Earn and so laden with their plunder they rowed across to the safe haven of their island in the safe knowledge that they would now be perfectly safe from any attempted recourse from their enemies.

An infuriated McNab of McNab, chieftain of the clan was maddened by the audacity of the Neishes. In the great clan hall he bellowed out to his attendant 12 sons "Bhin oidche an oidche, nan ghillean an ghillean" which being translated meant "The night is the night, if the lads are lads". The 12 sons shouldered a large boat (for they knew that the would be unable to acquire one over the Hill) and set off on the long march up Ardeonaig Glen on the route favoured for many years by the cattle drovers on the way to the Crieff Tryst, and thence down Glentarken to Loch Earn. The celebrating Neishes totally unsuspecting of any possible visitation were by this time getting somewhat drowsy as the McNabs stealthily paddled there way across to the little island Big John McNab the leader of the little band knocked at the door of the Neish stronghold. "Who is there?" came the query from inside. "Who would you not like to see?" asked McNab. "Smooth John McNab!", came the drunken response. "Smooth John McNab it is!" cried the oldest of the McNab brothers as he led the charge into the castle.

It was a massacre and all perished save a small boy who managed to swim ashore unnoticed. The McNabs decapitated their victims placing the gory trophies in a sack and proceeded back up the Glen towards Killin. The boat was abandoned en route and it is said that the remains lay there for all to see for many a long day. On reaching home, Iain Min or Smooth John entered his ancestral home where his father sat at the long wooden dining table with a number of his supporters. With a flamboyant gesture Iain Min emptied the sack and out tumbled the heads of their dreaded enemies. The old man turned to his son and said loudly in Gaelic, "The night was the night, and the lads were the lads!"

It is said that the sole survivor of the massacre, the young lad who swam to the shore is the sole ancestor of all the Neishes currently alive.

The Murder of Drummond Earnoch

The names of the Clans of Upper Strathearn include apart from the powerful Murrays and Drummonds, those of the McNabs, McLarens, McGregors and Grahams. For many years the most powerful Clan locally were the Drummonds whose titular head was Lord Drummond Earl and later Duke of Perth. When James VI had married the Danish Princess Anne in October 1589 Patrick Drummond as Steward of Strathearn and Chief Forester to the King's Royal Forest of Glen Artney was given the job of ensuring that the countless celebrations of the marriage had copious amounts of venison from the Royal Forest. Task was delegated to the laird's forester John Drummond Earnoch who with his men set off on their mission. In the course of their duties they came across some poachers. History records that they were possibly McGregors from close by but there is a tradition that the poachers were in fact McDonalds from Glencoe who were regarded in the Strath as a troublesome crew.

Drummond Earnoch in accord with the violence associated with the times did not hesitate in punishing the poachers. They were sent on their way having had their ears chopped off.

The McGregors, indeed if that's who it was, determined on retribution. It is alleged that these McGregors were of the branch of the Clan known as Children of the Mist and descended from one Duncan Laudasach. Their reputation was at stake and they sought out Drummond Earnoch. The poor forester was murdered and his body decapitated. Nearby on the southern shores of Loch Earn dwelt Stewart of Ardvorlich whose wife happened to be the sister of the murdered forester. Unaware of the ghastly crime that had been perpetrated she welcomed the murderers when they knocked on her door seeking refreshment. As is the custom of the Highlands no such request could be refused and she bad them enter. The Lady of Ardvorlich placed as an interim measure some bread and cheese on the table and excused herself to go and seek out something more substantial for her hungry guests. When she returned, to her horror there on the table was the dripping head of her brother with the bread and cheese stuffed into his mouth. The demented woman ran screaming from the house and took off into the hills that climb skyward towards the massive Ben Vorlich to the south. For several days she wandered hither and thither in a distracted way. She was spotted by some of the local women returning with their cattle to their sheilings, hiding in the thick bushes that grew abundantly on the verdant slopes. It was her husband who eventually the next day managed to persuade the poor woman to come home. The poor woman was pregnant at the time. Fortunately her son James Stewart was delivered safely a short time afterwards.

There was as a strange follow on to the murder of Drummond Earnoch and something which points the finger of blame fairly firmly towards the McGregors as being the culprits It is said that the murderers after leaving Ardvorlich made there way westwards towards the McGregor lands at nearby Balquhidder. Here on Loch Voil dwelt the chief's brother Iain dubh. Iain was a landowner of some substance and lived on Inch McGregor or McGregor's Island on the loch. Iain dubh sent for his brother the Clan Chief, Alasdair who organised a ceremony on the Sunday in the church at

Balquhidder, eaglais-beag. The gory head of Drummond Earnoch was placed on the alter and Chief Alasdair walked up and placed his right hand upon it and vowed to protect the murderers thus sharing in their guilt. Each member of the clan present then replicated their chief's action and walked up to the head, laid their hand upon it and repeated the vow.

This led to all the landlords of the district including Drummond, Atholl and Murray of Tullibardine being given a Commission to seek out and detain the Chief of the McGregors, Alasdair of Glenstrae, his brother Iain dubh, two of his uncles and a hundred and thirty five clansmen. This virtually gave those being granted the Commission to act accordingly and catch and execute the miscreants. The result was a period of violent retribution carried out by the Drummonds and Stewarts. Thirty-seven were slain at Invernenty and another twelve hanged on an oak tree nearby which, rumour hath, did never bear an acorn again!

The Gravestones of Ardvorlich

The twisting, narrow road down the south side of Loch Earn seems a world apart from its counterpart on the other side of the Loch. As one proceeds from St Fillans towards Ardvorlich you pass an intriguing memorial stone (OS ref NN 653 234) beside the Loch and just below the old croft of Coillemhor. The stone carries the inscription *"This stone marks the place of interment of Major James Stewart afterwards removed to the family vault at Dundurn died about 1660"*. Who was James Stewart and what were the reasons behind his corpse being buried at this spot? His mother was the poor woman who had been traumatised by being shown the gory head of her brother Drummond Earnoch at Ardvorlich those years back. James Stewart had apparently during his lifetime fallen foul of some of his neighbouring clans including the Grahams and not surprisingly the McGregors! Despite a lifetime of violence Stewart died in his bed and after the traditional wake attended by his clansmen retainers, the cortege set off eastwards along a winding track (above the route of the current loch side road) for the family vault at the old kirk of Dundurn by what is now the village of St Fillans. Such was the enmity against the deceased even in death that a plot had been hatched to way lay the party and desecrate the body. The party stopped above Coillemhor (the big wood) and dropped down to the loch side where they secretly buried the body. The schemes of James Stewart's enemies had been thwarted! Later when things had settled down his body was exhumed and the procession continued to Dundurn where he was laid to rest.

The violence of the times in the Highlands has spawned many legends and tales. A study of our history reveals that within the gaedhealteachd there were countless feuds and clashes between the various clans. The position in Strathearn was no different from elsewhere. There had been a great deal of enmity between the Stewarts and the MacDonalds of Glencoe. This had arisen from the murder of John Stewart of Strathgarry in Atholl by the MacDonalds and as a result the combined strength of the Stewarts of Appin, Atholl and Ardvorlich swept into the Glen and murdered the MacDonald chief and his son. Such an act had to be avenged and a party of seven MacDonald's, guided by a McGregor of nearby Glen Dochart raided Ardvorlich with the intention of burning down the house and the thatched biggins surrounding it. James Stewart of Ardvorlich had taken refuge in a cave just above St Fillans and there had a dream when he envisaged rats gnawing at the foundations of his home across the Loch Three times he had the same dream and so, feeling that it must be some kind of warning set off to determine for himself. When he arrived at Ardvorlich he saw a man with a lighted torch trying to set alight the thatch of the dairy. He took aim with his gun and shot the MacDonald attacker dead.

By this time some of his own men had arrived and the rest of the raiders were slain. The McGregor guide who was known as M'Clerich or Clark made his escape but was caught in a nearby wood and killed. That wood to this day is known as Clark's Wood or Coille Chlerich. The bodies of the attackers were buried in a mass grave by the loch side. When the present road was being constructed many years later the bodies were dug up and reburied nearby. A stone was erected to this effect carrying the inscription *"Near this spot we reinterred the bodies of 7 McDonalds killed when attempting to harry Ardvorlich. Anno Domini 1620"*.

St Fillan and his bell

St Fillan was an eighth century Irish born Saint who is believed to have lived near Loch Dochart which lies at the west end of the Glen of the same name near the present day village of Crianlarich. The importance of the saint is that five of his relics are still with us providing a tangible link with the past. The keepers of these relics were the stewards or "deor" in Gaelic which gives us the name Dewar still found throughout this part of Perthshire. The relics included his crozier head, the "quigrich" in its 14th century filigree case. This was returned some years ago from Canada where it had found its way. The other relic is the bronze bell of St Fillan which was retrieved from the ancient Priory of St Fillans near Crianlarich. These are now housed in the splendid new Museum of Scotland in Edinburgh.

Who then was St Fillan? He is believed to have come from ancient Celtic royal stock and that his mother was Kentigerna, a Princess of Ulster who had married into the royal family of the Kingdom of Dalriada which occupied at that time both Ulster and the west of Scotland in what is now Argyll. Legend has it that he had been born with a facial deformity and had been thrown into a river to drown by his father. It transpired that Fillan was rescued by Christian monks who cared for him thereafter. He did not lose touch with his mother and when he was older mother and son moved across the water to Scotland as Christian missionaries. Kentigerna settled on

Inchcaillach on Loch Lomond where she founded a nunnery whilst Fillan headed north up Glen Falloch from Loch Lomondside to Crianlarich and Glen Dochart.

After a life time of good works St Fillan died but by this time a Priory named after him had been established in what is now named Strathfillan. The bell of the Priory is the subject of legend. It was reputed to have miraculous powers and when the Prior required it, it flew by its own volition to wherever required! Apparently it was shot at by a stranger to Glen Dochart whilst in full flight and was brought to the ground. The crack you see in the museum is believed to be as a result of this incident all those years ago!

It was St Fillans arm bone that Bruce brought to the field of Bannockburn from its sanctuary by the Abbot of Inchaffrey. Inchaffrey lies some two miles to the east of Crieff and the somewhat decrepit remains can be found next to a somewhat incongruous modern dwelling. Indeed it is told that the Abbot who actually brought it to the field had little faith in Bruce's chances and left the bone out of it's casket. As the King on the eve of battle gathered with his knights at the alter to pray for victory, the lid flew open to reveal the relic. An astounded Abbot told the King that he had left the arm bone back in Perthshire. The fact that it had appeared was seen as a miracle and an omen for victory, which of course it was!

The reason that the arm was regarded as particularly important is that during the Saint's lifetime, a servant had observed a light coming from his cell. Knowing that he did not possess any candles, the servant opened the door to find Fillan illuminating the darkness by a light emanating from his left arm. When he died the arm was cut off and preserved.

St Fillan's bell was used from about the 17th century as a cure for persons regarded as not being in their right mind. These people were brought to a pool near St Fillan's grave, tied with a rope and thrown into the water before being pulled out. They were then taken back to the churchyard, tied to a large stone, covered with hay and the bell put on their head! They were then left all night. When the relatives returned back next day, if the ropes were then loose, the person was reputedly cured! Despite being stolen by a sassenach visitor, the bell was returned to Scotland and is on display with the crozier in the Museum of Scotland in Edinburgh. The pool is known as the Holy Pool of St Fillan and is situated about a mile and a half from Tyndrum. Apart from the rituals when the mentally sick were treated, the pool saw people coming there from all over seeking a miracle cure for a variety of ailments. After bathing in the waters each person gathered nine stones from the pool and walked to the top of the hillock beside it. On the hillock were three cairns and round each cairn the patient walked three times clockwise, the magical direction of the Gaels. At the end of each rotation one stone would be deposited on the cairn and at the finish of the three turns do likewise to the next two cairns. Onto the cairn he or she would throw the part of his clothing, which covered the afflicted part of their body.

The McGregors and of course Rob Roy!

The rise to stardom of Ewan McGregor, the lad from Crieff is welcome and well deserved. His ancestor, a certain Rob Roy McGregor had achieved fame, nay notoriety far beyond the confines of the Strath. It was on the 7th of March 1671 that one "Donald McGregor in Glengyll, Parish of Callander, upon the certificate of the Minister thereof and Margaret Campbell, son, baptised Robert." This was the arrival of the lad who was to make his mark on the countryside about, the famous or perhaps infamous Rob Roy McGregor!

Rob Roy was so called from the fiery colour of his hair. His pedigree perhaps explains why Rob made more than a little impression on Strathearn! His father Lt Col Donald McGregor of Glengyle was an army officer in the army of King Charles ll and his wife Margaret Campbell was a half sister of the notorious Campbell of Glenlyon who was responsible for the massacre of Glencoe! With such antecedents how could he have failed to make his mark on our history! Glengyle was over the hills south of Inverlochlarig near Loch Katrine. Later when these lands were taken over by the Duke of Montrose the lease was renewed to one Gregor Glun Dhu who purchased the land and became the first chief who owned the land on which he lived (The Braes of Balquhidder, Beauchamp, 1981). Rob Roy's father Donald was imprisoned in Edinburgh for being an ardent Jacobite having fought at Killiecrankie in support of James Vll as well as having a history of being an expert cattle "lifter". At this time in the Highlands wealth was mainly adjudged by the number of cattle or sheep in one's possession. The source of acquisition was not discussed provided it was not from your own clan. Rob Roy's father had been captured whilst on one such cattle raid on the lands of Kilmaronock, near Drymen.

Donald was granted his release after signing an oath of loyalty to King William and payment of a ransom. It was at this time that a scheme derived from an idea of Lord Breadalbane that a system of "watches" be set up by the various lairds who had suffered from these cattle raids. The idea was that these vigilantes would form a protective band paid for by the lairds to ensure that no cattle were stolen as had been happening for decades. The Government was petitioned and approval received.

Donald McGregor of Glengyle and his cousin Archibald McGregor of Kilmanan became joint commanders of the Highland Watch. One of the privileges was the right to bear arms. Indeed it was from this origin that the regiment called the Black Watch was formed in 1740.

Young Rob had followed on the family tradition when at the age of twenty and to relieve a family financial crisis after the release of his father captured some 250 beasts being driven home from the Balloch Fair. Shortly after this incident Rob secured the tenancy of Monachyle Tuarach from the Marquis of Atholl. This was at the place where Loch Doine joins with Loch Voil (OS ref NN 477 192). It was not the most ideal of locations for farming being low lying and subject to flooding as well as having a northerly exposure. For a while the cattle rustler became a sheep farmer. In 1693 he married his cousin Mary McGregor of Comar that lay to the west on the slopes of Ben Lomond. That year his father died. His mother had pre-deceased him by two years. John, Rob's older brother now became chief of the Dougal Ceir sept of the Clan McGregor whilst Rob took over the Captaincy of the powerful Highland Watch.

It was at this time that a ban was placed on the McGregor name. Rob adopted his mother's name of Campbell. Notwithstanding this, his "Business" expanded and became exceedingly lucrative. Undoubtedly it now operated as something of a protection racket and combined with his cattle dealing operations ensured a prosperous existence.

Rob Roy was a regular attender at the Michaelmas Tryst in Crieff, which had become the country's premier sale of cattle with drovers arriving in Strathearn from all over the Highlands, the northeast and the north. In 1714, the time of the first Jacobite Uprising, the Government detailed a detachment of Hanoverian troops to deal with any disquiet that might arise in the town. The first incident occurred when a number of MacDonalds were involved in consuming amounts of illegal whisky (ie no duty had been paid on it) when a "gauger" or exciseman intervened and confiscated the lot. The MacDonalds desisted from any action at the time on account of the close presence of the Hanoverian troops. That night however they entered the house of the exciseman and hauling him out of bed forced him to his knees, cut off his right ear and made him drink the health of the Jacobite James Vlll in similar whisky to that which had been confiscated earlier in the day. Despite a search by the soldiers throughout Crieff, the perpetrators of the deed were, surprise, surprise, not found.

It happened that Rob Roy was also in Crieff at this time. Having had a good laugh at the above incident, he assembled all his clansmen secretly in a close by field on a clear moon light night. Thirty of his McGregors assembled and when the parish bell rang the hour at mid night, they were led by Rob to the Cross of Crieff by the town hall and encircled it. A cask of untaxed whisky was broached and filling their quaichs, Rob, himself called upon them to drink a toast to the health of His Majesty, King James the Eighth, with all honours. This was done amongst ringing cheers, which roused the town (Porteous, 1912), and Rob then kept up the revelry for some time longer by drinking to the various nobles who had upheld the cause. "*Success to Tullibardine and confusion to Montrose*" together with various other toasts. As the Hanoverian troops were now assembling, Rob thought it time to end the display so he gave a final toast "*the health to those honest and brave fellows who cut off the gadger's ear*" and with those last words the McGregors hastened out of town and dispersed!

Rob Roy's life was the subject of Scott's novel of that name and in more recent years the film with Irishman Liam Neeson as Rob was shot partly in the Strath which seems quite apposite! Rob physically was described (*Braes of Balquhidder*, Beauchamp, 1981) as being "*a stocky, stalwart powerful looking fellow, not very tall because of his shortish legs but with exceptionally long arms which gave him a great advantage when he came to using a sword, he could tie his garters two inches below the knee without stooping. He had red hair, red hairy arms and legs and penetrating blue eyes*".

Those who have seen the Schotz statue of Rob Roy outside the Albert Hall in Stirling will agree that the above description has been well copied in bronze.

Rob Roy, born at Glengyle in the Parish of Callander, at the north west end of Loch Katrine, died at Inverlochlarig a mere 5 miles as the crow flies from his birth place over the peak of Stob a' Choin at the foot of the glen to the west of Balquhidder. He was buried in the churchyard of Balquhidder Kirk. The tales of his hectic life are well and truly embedded in our Scottish folklore.

Ochtertyre – astronomy – plague – wolves and a massacre

Many of you will have travelled by Stagecoach. No, not that carriage made famous in the John Ford movie of that name but that gaily coloured omnibus that plies the many routes throughout Scotland or even as far away as England or the US! The co founder of the Stagecoach multi national bus company, Brian Soutar, multi millionaire and espouser of causes lives outside Crieff on that house on the hill, namely Ochtertyre, a Georgian mansion of classic proportions overlooking the Comrie Road, Ochtertyre Loch and that delightfully named Castle Cluggie. The following extract is taken from an article written about 1880 and archived in the Sandeman Papers in the AK Bell Library, Perth.

"*The mansion house of Ochtertyre was built towards the end of the last century by Sir William Murray on a site at once commanding and well protected and in the midst of luxuriant surroundings of mountain and forest, field and lake. Sir Patrick Murray succeeded to the estate in 1800. He was a member of the Scottish Bar and took an active part in public affairs and twice represented the City of Edinburgh in Parliament. He had a taste for landscape gardening, and by the many improvements on his estate he taught the surrounding proprietors how to beautify and enrich their grounds. To him is the district indebted for the many fine public highways leading in many directions most of which were made in the first decade of this century under his personal supervision. His son Sir William Keith Murray succeeded him in 1837. In 1829 he published* Sketches of Scenes in Scotland, *being a series of lithograph landscape drawings in which he showed high artistic skill. He also studied astronomy and in 1852 erected a fine observatory a little to the west of the mansion house and behind the old castle (Cluggie). It contained two splendid telescopes. One of them was a 13' equatorial with a 9' object glass with clockwork* attachment; the other was an 8.5 foot Munich equatorial having a 6-8-10 object glass. There was also the necessary transit instruments and clocks. The roofs were constructed to run round on railway wheels and were driven by tiller wheels and ropes. There was a platform on the south side of the observatory where smaller telescopes were occasionally placed when the moon or planets were in favourable positions for being seen. Many people from the surrounding villages and districts were specially invited to feast their eyes on these far away worlds. The observatory was dismantled a short time after his death and the largest of the telescopes is now at Gilmorehill, Glasgow and known as the Ochtertyre telescope.

Sir William was also an accomplished musician and the Ochtertyre concerts were thoroughly enjoyable. The worthy Baronet was most anxious to do his utmost for the benefit of his fellow men, and his beautiful grounds were open to all and people were welcome to the observatory at all times. He died 16th October 1861 very greatly lamented. Sir Patrick Keith Murray the present baronet was a Captain in the Grenadier Guards and retired about the time of his father's death.

There are several fine cascades on the estate, the three principal ones being within easy walking distance of Crieff – namely Spout Buick, Spout Barvick and the Falls of Kelty. Fine walks lead to all these interesting places on the grounds, where the utmost diversity of scenery is found, to all of which the worthy Baronet allows the people to roam at will. Those who enjoy these great privileges are expected to avoid destroying the plants and flowers which bloom so invitingly around.

At the east end of the Serpentine Lake is St Serf's Well. St Serf was the patron saint of the parish of Monzievaird. In old times St Serf's annual market was held on 11th July on the moor which then extended from the Well to Old Church. Last century the people were wont on Lammas day to go and drink at the Well and it was customary to throw white stones, spoons and rags therein as an earnest belief in the virtues of the water. An old chronicle states 'It has been useful for a patient taking a tub of it, and immediately plunging his arms into it, a cure followed.'

In the time of Charles l , the plague visited the district and many died in the parish. The plague stricken were kept in huts by themselves at the West End of the Loch of Ochtertyre. Attendants called cleansers waited upon the diseased giving them food and other necessaries. In windy weather the cleansers laid the food &c., on the wind side of the huts for the sick to come and take it. Acts of Parliament were passed in 1645 directing that public contributions be collected for the benefit of the plague-stricken in the parishes of Crieff, Monzievaird and Comrie. The keeper of the public magazine at Perth was instructed to give four-score balls of meal for the use of these parishes. Orders were also issued for voluntary contributions to be collected in the parishes unvisited by he plague and unburned in Perthshire. The mounds or graves of those who perished at Monzievaird are still visible and marked on the Government survey map a little to the West of the Loch.

One day during the time of the plague the watchers witnessed a wolf hunt. A number of armed men had found two wolves in the wood of Trowan about a mile Southwards and pursuing them Northwards passed the West end of the loch away *to the hills where the animals were killed. They were the last heard of in the district. It is probable they were the last of their kind in Scotland."*

It would remiss to end this brief synopsis of the history of Ochtertyre without mentioning two important aspects in the history of this elegant mansion and its adjoining estate. The family of Murray incumbent in Ochtertyre for many a long year were often in conflict with their immediate neighbours, the powerful Drummond family of Drummond Castle. In 1511, the old church of Monzievaird was the scene of a dreadful tragedy. There had long been a bitter feud between the two families and at that time tension had been exacerbated by the Murrays exacting tithes (land taxes) from the Drummonds and carrying off spoil from their lands. They met at length at length at Knock Mary, the hill south of the Earn above the Braidhaugh where the Drummonds were assisted by the McRobbies from the Loch of Balloch area. The Drummonds were vanquished and the Murrays returned home with the spoils of their foes. The Drummonds were joined by Campbell of Dunstaffnage and a large body of his clansmen. Campbell had come to avenge the death of his father in law, whom, with his two sons, had been killed by the Murrays. Thus strengthened the Drummonds pursued the Murrays, who, afraid to risk a new engagement sought refuge in the Kirk of Monzievaird; into which they also brought their wives and children. A Drummond pursuer having come within a musket-shot of the church, and a Murray unable to restrain himself, fired at him. This revealed their refuge, and of course increased the passion of their pursuers for revenge. They surrounded the church, and summoned the Murrays to surrender. They answered with a haughty defiance. The besiegers then called for fire; and the church, being thatched with heather, became an easy and a speedy prey to the devouring element. One hundred and sixty men, with their wives and children, were burned to death. Only one of the Murrays within escaped, and that through the connivance of a Drummond to whom he had done a favour. James IV, promptly brought the Drummonds to a strict reckoning for this outrage. The Master of Drummond and several of his followers were apprehended and brought to trial; and, being found guilty of this massacre, were condemned and executed at Stirling.

The site of the massacre was not the ruined kirk located in the old Monzievaird burial ground near the Quoigs Cottages north of the Crieff/Comrie road but that of the present Murray family Mausoleum located within the Ochtertyre Estate on the left hand side just north of the Granite Lodge entranceway. This is within private ground with no public access. When the Mausoleum was being built, traces of the burning were found whilst digging the founds. A quantity of charred wood was discovered, the remains of the original fabric as well as a very large quantity of calcined bones. *"It occupied many days to remove them to another part of the churchyard. Some of them were of great size, and those which were so were all found near the west wall of the Mausoleum, where it is believed the door of the church stood. Towards the east of the building, and near the door of the Mausoleum, the bones have generally been small. This is, probably, accounted for by supposing that the women and children were placed farthest from the door of the church, and that it was guarded by the strongest and bravest men of the Clan. The bones seem to have been buried where they lay"*. The cairn raised to mark the resting place of the slain still remains close beside the Mausoleum.

Chapter 12

Our Davy

General Sir David Baird of Ferntower

There are a number of people who over the centuries have left their impact on Strathearn. One who memory stands out more than most is that of Sir David Baird who resided at Ferntower near Crieff in his retirement from a memorable career in the British Army. A contemporary of Wellington, the two had little in common. The former the arrogant patrician, the latter the product of an Edinburgh merchant middle class. When asked to describe Davy, Wellesley aka The Duke of Wellington, who seemed somewhat put out by Baird's "one of the boys" approach to soldiering, snapped *"Baird was a gallant, hard headed officer but he had no talent, no tact, had an unpredictable temper and by past experience was unfitted to govern the natives."* Baird's mother is reported as saying *"Lord help the chiel that's chained to our Davy!"*

Therein lies the background to a soldier who achieved great success but because of his basic approach to soldiering upset the existing establishment who ran Britain's class rigid military. His entry was not by the privileged system of buying commissions but by fighting his way up by merit and by power of personality and character. His experience in India and in Seringapatam where he led from the front were followed by battles in Egypt, The Cape of Good Hope and finally in Spain where again his experience, ability and advice were ignored to the cost of the British army saw him retire somewhat disillusioned. According to Haley (Our Davy, Bullfinch) Baird retired to Ferntower in Crieff having married Miss Ann Campbell Preston of an old Scottish family. Baird's portrait by Raeburn hangs in the Crieff Hydro, a fitting place for a man who came late to the Strath but attained the regard and respect of the local people. His wife was a strong character and Baird is reported as saying *"I could command 10,000 men yet I cannot command one woman"*.

Ferntower at Baird's time was a large spread out estate covering much of the area around Crieff. The Estate was sold in 1911 and information kindly provided by the late Bob Torrens of Crieff shows details of the sale at that time. It encompassed some 3300 acres of land in total. Ferntower itself included the mansion house, offices and lodges and lay in what is now

102

Ferntower House, once the home of General Sir David Baird,
was demolished in the 1950s.

Crieff Golf Course. The lodges are still there but the house itself was demolished by the army in the 1950s. It lay at what is now the upper part of the Ferntower course and until recently part of the stable block was still occupied. Included within the policies were the Crieffvechter farms, Colony, Greenhead, Peathills, Tomaknock, Laker and Callum's Hill Quarry. The estate also encompassed Lochlane to the south of Crieff on the back road to Comrie. Apart from the Lochlanes it included Knockieston, the pendicle at Dallerie and various shootings. The Madderty part of the Estate included Parkside, Westbank, Muirmouth, Cargates, Woodburn, Newraw, Muirend, Craig and the land at St Davids named of course after Davy! At the time of the sale the occupant of Mansion house was Dr T H Meikle of Hydro fame.

The purchase for the Hydro of much of Ferntower no doubt helped them to develop much over the years to the benefit of the town and its citizens. The present Crieff Golf Club in fact rents the course from the Hydro and its development and position as a prime attraction to the golfing fraternity and tourists should not be overlooked.

The sales particulars prepared by the Agents Messrs T & R B Ranken of Edinburgh are a fund of historically fascinating information. We glean from them that the Mansion House was in excellent order and contains an Entrance Hall, Dining Room, Double Drawing Room, Two sitting Rooms, Twelve Bedrooms, Two Dressing Rooms and ample Servants' Accommodation. From an earlier census account we discover that at one time eight gardeners looked after the grounds!

The Estate was not devoid of game. In the list of sale are tables of game killed in the period 1908 to 1911. They included roe deer, black game, capercailzie, pheasants, partridges, woodcock, snipe, wild duck, golden plover, hares and rabbits. In the period listed some 129 salmon were taken in the waters of the Estate.

One year after his marriage Baird was planning to extend Ferntower. The Peninsula Generals were rewarded in 1814 after the defeat of Napoleon with Peerages and pensions of some two thousand pounds per annum. David Baird despite a claim received not even a reply. He spent time as a Governor in Ireland and in charge of the army there. He was greatly moved by the poverty of the people and duly recorded his findings. He retired thereafter to Ferntower He died at Crieff after sustaining injuries on a fall from his horse. He was buried in Strathearn but his body was later reinterred at Culross in Fife, the traditional resting place of his wife's family.

Davy Baird's memory is encapsulated in the Baird Monument erected on the ancient site of Tom na Chastel that was on the Estate. It is a replica of Cleopatra's Needle and on it is inscribed the battles of Davy Baird, a man of the people. It remains a favourite walk for locals and visitors alike. A fitting tribute to a man from Edinburgh who found peace at last in the quiet Strath which gave him so much pleasure in the autumn of his life.

"A warrior without fear or reproach, intending no guile and believing in no treachery. Throughout his life he made many friends and never lost the esteem he once acquired. He was not given to talk of his own services and exploits and was ever ready to bear testimony to the deeds of others. He thought he had been treated with neglect and inadequately rewarded, but he rejoiced when his comrades were successful; and though his application for a peerage was passed over without the courtesy of an answer, he was never heard to insinuate that those preferred were not deserving". (J W Cole.)

Chapter 13

Crieff in the Second World War

Introduction

This is the transcription of an interview undertaken with an old Crieff resident as part of an Open University course in oral history in 1998. The interviewer is referred to as "A" whilst the interviewee is referred to as "B". The interview reveals some interesting facts about the town, its permanent occupants and those there by the necessity of war.

The interview

A: Could we start by telling when and where you were born?

B: On the — -1920 opposite the police station in King Street, Crieff. We then moved up to the High Street to that big block, you know? We stayed there until I was 12. My father was a nurseryman at Gavelbeg Nursery and we lived in the wee cottage down the Lane 'till after the war. In 1947 we moved to the new houses they built at Alligan. It became too big for me and I moved here about '94.

A: You went to school here in Crieff?

B: I went to the Primary School. It was the only school there was in the town. My gran and my mother as well as my brother all went there. A lot of alterations were done when my mother was there; they added the gym and the classrooms at the back. I left in 1937. Of course by that time it was a secondary school as well, up to third year.

A: What about the houses in Crieff?

B: A big difference. A lot were built after the War. There were no houses down below Broich Road, none in Hollybush or the Turret. Sauchie was the first scheme to be built.

A: Where did most of the people come from, from Crieff?

105

B: After the War, there were a lot from outside. There have been more and more of these incomers. A call them the "white settlers"! (*Laugh*). Ye canny git a seat in the library for them aw coontin their stocks and shares!

A: Did the War bring changes to the work people did in the town? What were the main changes you saw regarding this?

B: You'll remember the old Cash and Carry when it was in Leadenflower; well that was Crerar's coach works. And of course the lemonade works was also there. Crerar was the man who started the buses in Crieff and of course he built the cinema. No just here but in Auchterarder and even Dunfermline! All over the place.

A: He was a well known person about the town then?

B: Oh yes, a nice lad Peter. I got on with him well. He built charabancs and the buses He started before I was at school. My auntie worked wi' him. She was a conductress. They went to Perth, Comrie, Dunning and Auchterarder. One and six to go to Perth and that was a return! He built buses in there. He bought Ruberslaw and brought people in from Aberdeen. They were all coachbuilders. You'll know auld John —— he was one. His son lives on Addison Terrace. Lots of Aberdonians. This was just before the war started. It was a big business. They also built speed boats. Lots o' people came to the works. At one time they employed over 30 men. An Englishman arrived. He was a panel beater. He stayed with my grannie. He opened a cycle shop in the Square. That was before they built the Mill shop.

A: What did you do when you left school?

B: Ah worked as a joiner with my uncle. He had come home from the First War and went to work as a boy with Sam Wilson. His workshop was near Frank Thomsons, the Ironmongers. Sam's daughter still lives out the Comrie Road. They did the work for Peter Crerar during the '20s and '30s. They started to build a garage where the Spar shop now is. Peter came up to them one day and said, "Stop! We are going to build a picture house and not a garage." That was the first picture house in Crieff. That would be about 1921.

A: You would have been a young man when the War broke out.

B: I was 18.

A: What was Crieff like at that time?

B: It was very quiet. That was in 1938. We knew it was coming. I tell you there were very good tourist association, hotel keepers and the like. They used to have gala day in the summertime and things like that. Of course 1938 was the year of Empire Exhibition at Bellahouston in Glasgow.

The Crieff Platoon of the Home Guard pictured about 1944 outside the Drill Hall in Commissioner Street.

I remember it fine for we had our holidays in Glasgow that year. That was when old Chamberlain had that bit of paper from Hitler saying it was not to be. We did not believe it for they came with conscription. If you joined the Territorial Army you were not to be conscripted. You needed to do three years. Two dozen of us headed for Perth. Into the bus and off to join up. The RASC . A place in Perth just next to the railway line. I was examined by the doctor. He said I am not going to take you. Can you come into Perth on Saturday night and bring your father with you. He said that they would not take me because of this leg. I had had polio when I was young. When I did go for my medical in July 1940, that was just one week after my birthday. I was 20. There were four of us went to Dundee. Six or seven doctors there looked at me, they wouldn't wear it. "Oh no we cant take you. Just carry on with your work." I worked as a joiner of course and we got a lot of work. My uncle taught woodwork up at Ardvreck School. We got work up there; ah say it was wheels within wheels. I remember however I think it was 1940, it came over the wireless one night, it was the Dunkirk time and Anthony Eden spoke. They were starting the Home Guard. Three of us joined up.

A: *Where about did they meet?*

B: The Drill hall where Cornerstone is now. The three of us went down. That was the start of it. Alec —— was younger than me and he worked with Frank Thomson in the wireless shop. Raymond —— was born the same day as me; he cheated and volunteered for the Air Force! He married and is now down in Brighton. That was the start of the Home Guard in 1940.

A: *What were your duties in the Home Guard in Crieff?*

B: You started off and we had nothing. I can always vouch for that. Pikestaffs, long tubes of steel with a pin stuck in the end of it. The only rifles we had were Lee Enfields from the Morrison's Academy OTC . These were left over from the First War. We had to use them. Of course by this time we had troops in Crieff. The first lot were a company of signals. They were based in the Hydro. They had come in 1939. That was when old Paddy —— came to Crieff, he came as a soldier. He married his wife and stayed on after the war. They used to come down to the town and parade to the Drill Hall. There were a couple of hundred of them. As soon as Dunkirk came they got shifted. The next thing we knew there were others coming in. They sent a lot of conscripts from Stonehaven. Nice blokes. Most were in the RASC. They took over Taylor's Institute School now the Legion. The school was empty at the time. They had moved it down to the Primary School. After that there came a battalion of the Inneskillen Fusiliers, a battalion of the Wiltshire Regiment and a battalion of the Cameronians. All regulars. The first instructors we had were from the Inniskillens. I always remember Sergeant Campbell, he was the nicest bloke you could meet. He taught me to shoot. His language wasn't good. But he was very helpful. They were based in the Institute. What we called the Crieff Hall where Meadow Motors used to be. The cookhouse was outside in the Market Park. There were troops down there. The Meadow Inn, there were troops in there and Nissan huts at the Bridgend. The Officers and the Cameronians were up in the Hydro. This was the early part of the war. In 1940. The First Battalion Brigade HQ was the Cultoquhay Hotel. Always was. From that time there was always a brigade of troops in Crieff.

A: *How did the locals react to so many soldiers being here?*

B : They got on very well with the soldiers. Where the library is, was made into a Church of Scotland canteen. Up the stairs there was a billiard table and a piano. They could always get a cup of tea. The women of the town cooked sausage and mash. There were always cigarettes available. Things we could nae get of course! After the Inniskillens, the next thing we had were the 52nd Lowland Division, two battalions of the HLI and another of the Cameronians. The came in and they were here for a while. They got shifted then they came back again. We also had Canadians in between that. They were all right. They fought amongst themselves but they never touched civilians. The women were as safe as houses with them. We also had the West Kents and some others. They were all over the town.

A : *Why do you think they sent so many troops to Crieff?*

B: I think every place had them but here it was such a central place. Of course you had to get them here and of we had to have the places to put them. When I think of it there were a lot. A brigade had three to four thousand men.

A: That is a lot when before the War the population of Crieff was only 5,000.

B: A lot of them were not from this area. The Highland Division were down in England. We had what they called the Y Division but they too disappeared after awhile and toured the world! Then we had the Canadians. I always remember the Canadians for our workshop was next to the Drill hall besides Barrington's Garage. This was across from the cookhouse. They used to sit on the stairs with all their food piled high up on one plate, the baked potatoes, pudding, the lot! They were quite nice blokes though. They were never short of things. You could always get things. You see things were rationed. Cigarettes were under the counter, you had to be in the know. You would only get ten at a time, but the Canadians got an issue of cigarettes, Camels Chesterfields, Sweet Avon. They got paid once a fortnight. Near the end of the second week when they were getting short, they would come into town with their gas mask cases filled with cigarettes. Six pence a packet! Had 3,000 stacked up in the house before long I knew I was getting them cheap. I helped with the Dances at the Drill Hall and the canteen. We ran them for charity on Saturday nights. Peter ——'s dad was the sergeant and me and the boys Rab and Johnnie and all the lads ran them, we raised a lot at that time.

A: When you were in the Home Guard, were there any incidents you remember?

B : There were lots (*laughter*), you don't want me to tell you everything! I can remember something big was happening and two Divisions came down from the North of Scotland. They sent us out to Gask School on Saturday and Sunday. We had sandwiches and our dixies. We tried to cook on the stove in the classroom but it would have taken a year to brew up and cook. One of the boys said there were lots of bricks lying outside so we went out and built a fire. We took some coals from the head mistresses room and piled on the logs. Black out or no black out we all had our tea outside. What a night! At the same time we had been told to keep our eye on the road passed the House of Gask which crosses the bridge where the main road to Perth goes. We blackened our faces and hid behind the hedge. A bloke on a bike came along and one of the lads jumped out. The poor man got such a fright that he leapt into the ditch. "Ah thought it wis an f——g ghost!", he blurted out. He had been down in Methven. I think he had had a wee drink though! These were the type of things that happened.

A: Despite all the troops stationed in the town, did it feel as if the war was along way away?

B: Well there was an airfield at Gask but that was to the east of the town. There was a stray bomb landed in Muthill .I wasn't out that night. I was in my bed. It must have been on its way back. It fell above the cemetery outside the village. My father was there. He was in the fire brigade down in Burrell Street. I think the only thing it killed were the rabbits!

A: *How about rationing and its effect on the morale of the town?*

B: We just accepted it. Things were hard, 2 ozs of tea a week and not much sugar, no bacon and little butcher meat. We got sausages occasionally. Sweets were rationed, clothes too and eggs were scarce. Towards the end of the War bread too was rationed. If you wanted a suit it was a years coupons. Shoes too were on coupons. Looking back however we all seemed to realise it had to be the way.

A: *On a personal note, did any family or friends fail to come back?*

B: Three who were at school with me, two were in the Air Force. One was in the Merchant Navy and was drowned in the landings in North Africa. That was in 1941 in Tunisia. One of my pals was in the Black Watch, he was killed at Dunkirk.

A: *Immediately after the war, what were the changes you noticed most?*

B: There weren't a lot of changes really. They started building down in the bottom of the town around Croftnappock and Alligan. That was where most of the new houses were built. A lot of the boys getting back from the war were getting married and were desperate for some place to live. A lot of the old houses were in poor condition. My father had finished at the nursery at Galvelbeg and we were put out. We had to move down to my Grannie's house in Galvelmore Street. We moved into the new house in 1947. It was the first time we had electric. The cottage had gas lighting and we had batteries for the wireless. The new houses were all built by local firms like Dodds and Devine. It also helped with jobs for a lot o the ones who had just come back. There had been an awful problem for the young ones before the War getting some where to Stay.

A: *How important was the railway in Crieff at this time?*

B : You could catch a train at eight minutes past eight in the morning and you could be in Glasgow at quarter to ten. Of course if you were going to Edinburgh you had to get into the back carriage which was dropped at Stirling and that was picked up and taken to Edinburgh. It was half past ten before you got to Edinburgh. It was five bob return to Glasgow or twenty five pence in present money! The last train back was ten past six at night.

A: *Who used these trains?*

B: Everybody. If you went by bus it was two and a half hours. Very few of course had motors. The roads were not like now. It was three hours by bus to Edinburgh. The trains were comfortable. Am no saying they were warm in wintertime but they were comfortable. You didn't have to rush. You would get to Buchanan Street early and get back in plenty of time at night.

A: *After the War were there many people from outside moving here?*

B: Och, they came and went. I would say that it was really only in the last twenty or so years that people started to move here from far away. That meant new houses at places like Nellfield on the old Academy hockey pitches, down at Turretbank, at Currachgreen on the site of the old nursery and at Hollybush Farm. The two old nurseries McOmish and McArras were taken over. That's where my father worked. That's where he served his time, Roys and McArras. McArra owned the big house up there.

A: *How does the town compare now with before?*

B: Ah would say this local government is a step for the worse. We are ruled from Perth and they could not care less about the place. It's the same all over Scotland.

A: *Of course up until the late seventies, Crieff had a Town Council. Was that very strong?*

B: Ah was on the Council. That took all our powers away. Even during the war we managed, everyone took part. If it snowed, the two horses would pull the plough to clear the streets. All the workman from the Council used to join in and clear the streets. They would start along Commissioner Street in the morning and when I got back from my work they had cleared all the snow. The pavements too were cleared. I think it was much better in those days.

A: *Is there anything that sticks out in your memory that happened in the town during the War?*

B: The Andrews Sisters came to the Drummond Arms. You'll no mind them? They were at the Empire in Glasgow at the time. They came into the Square and the crowds were everywhere. It was about then they built the prisoner of war camp at Cultybraggan. It was for German prisoners. I remembered two escaped one night and we were called out. We went out the Comrie Road and down by the river. But we missed them. They had gone down the other side. They reached Muthill station the next day but they gave themselves up. They were starving. At that time there were no problems with them. They were mainly U-Boat crews. And of course there were the Italians. They had huts down at the Catholic School. They had more freedom than the Germans. In fact I used to come down the Perth Road every morning about eight o'clock going to my work. We lived up there at the time. I used to meet this Italian in his battle dress and his big purple hat. He was working at the Hollybush Farm. He was a farmer back in Italy and was as happy as Larry. I don't think the Italians were very happy about the War. I remember I used to shout to him each morning, "Morning Guisepie!" The Italians were happy here in Crieff, we didn't think of them as an enemy.

A: *What about the Germans in Cultybraggan?*

B: That was a different kettle of fish. Most of them were from the U-Boats and other prisoners we didn't know much about. There was a murder there. There was an article in the *Herald* about it a few years back. We didn't know what happened. Ah had a pal in the Cameronians. They were ootside at the time. They were not allowed to go in. They stayed roond the perimeter. Apparently they hung a bloke from a cistern. He was supposedly giving information. It was all hushed up.

A: *Going back to the Hydro. Was it requisitioned?*

B: Right from 1939. The Signal Corps were there and the Poles came in for a while as well as the Cameronians. It was a limited company and I think they got money back after the War.

A: *Any other places commandeered?*

B: They took over the Games Park. The bases for the Nissan huts are still there. When they were built they went right up the King Street side and right round the park. They were just corrugated iron with two stoves. No very comfortable.

A: *What about the changes in the shops after the War?*

B : We didn't of course have any supermarkets. Lowe's was in Crieff at West High Street, the Coop was where the arcade is now and they had a butchers shop at the Cross where the camera shop is now. There was Coopers and a Lipton's in the High Street. They were grocer's shops. There were other grocers as well. Camerons a licences grocers was next to the library where the antique shop is. McEwans had another big grocers shop in the Square and down King Street was another one. There were far more butchers shops. There were four or five, now we have only one. There were four fish shops after the War. John Lowe's had been in West High Street for a hundred years before it became a sweetie shop.

A: *Do you notice a change in hotels and the like since the War?*

B: Oh it was a different set than it is now. There were all these hotels in the Square, The Drummond Arms, The Ancaster and the Glenburn. Of course Academy House was board residence and out the Comrie Road there was the Birches Hotel and Balmennoch was the Grampian Hill Hydropathic. It burned down and two people were burned to death. Wee Mr —— the owner was jailed for two years, he was the nicest wee man you could wish to meet! And the Towers that was also a board residence. The hotels up the Perth Road were houses before the War that is except the Kingarth. Then of course there were the pubs, the Pretoria, The Star and the Station. The one they call the Strathearn used to be the Commercial.

A: How did most of the holidaymakers travel to Crieff?

B: By train and by bus. Not like now when everyone has a car. It was a busy station in those days. The first train was in at quarter to seven. That brought your papers and the mail. Then there was one at eight o'clock and then nine o'clock. There was a separate line from Perth too. A lot of trains came in and out and of course there were a lot of goods trains. When the cattle market at the Gallowhill was on I've seen a huge train loading the cattle and taking them away. That finished after the War. Of course there was Morgan's saw mill at the Turret and of course McAinsh's. He had their mill at Balgowan and a workshop in Crieff down the School Wynd. He was in Crieff for a long time and employed joiners who made bogies and a lot of other things as well. He had mills all over including Ireland but his office was in Crieff down Drummawhandie.

The timber was sent out from the goods station where the car park is now. In would come wagons with coal six days a week. All ways it was very busy. There were two lorries delivering around the place. I remember my Grannie had a man staying with her who worked there and I used to take his breakfast down to him on Saturday mornings. He started very early unloading the wagons. The Hydro had a lot of people arriving on holiday. Before the War they had a charabanc pulled by horses which used to meet the trains and take the guests up the hill. After the War they had a bus and a big car. All gone.

A: There are a lot of empty churches in the town. You must have seen changes there?

B: A lot when you think back. I belonged to St Columbas the Episcopal Church. It's changed too. The did away with the original church and built a new one. I didn't like that. There was the West Parish Church, the South Parish Church, St Andrews and St Michaels. All Church of Scotland. The Baptist Church was in Addison Terrace. It's still there. The Catholic chapel was down Ford Road. It has altered a wee bit. Where the St Johnstone Club is was the Episcopal School before the War. They had a separate school. They had two teachers. After it was closed it became a church hall. Then there was the Salvation Army before the War. We used to go along to their film shows. They had a hall where the library is. In the summer they used to play in the Square. Some of their people lived in a house they owned down Addison Terrace.

A: Before the days of television, what did most people in the town do for entertainment?

B: The cinema. There were two picture houses in the town. The main one in High Street and the Ritz up Strathearn Terrace in Academy Hall, that was Porteous Hall. It was made into a cinema in 1938. During the War years they made a fortune. I've seen on a Saturday night if there was a good picture on, a queue for the second house right down to where the garage is. When there were 3,000 troops around, they were always busy. It was nine pence to get in.

A: *What else did people do?*

B: There were dances. Or you could listen to the wireless. Before the War a lot of the houses didn't have electricity and used batteries. The dances were in the Porteous Hall before it became a picture house and also in the Masonic hall which they did up. And also the Drill hall.

A: *You have lived in Crieff all your life. You have seen many changes. For better or for worse?*

B: People have better living conditions and there is more money around. Everything nowadays is in a rush. We don't seem to have as much freedom of choice. They have taken away much of our local control. When I was on the Council we could make decisions there and then. Not now! We can't even decide when we will have our local holidays! The Town Council was good balance for Crieff. There were no cliques or groups. It as not political, we were all independents in those days the last Provost was D——, he was a school master in the Catholic School. They were a great bunch. Every one worked hard. If you did some thing that upset people you got it in the street the next day! You couldn't get away! When they changed it we had two separate Councils. It was ridiculous. Ah blame the Tories. It wisnae needed. My years on the Council were satisfying. You got a chance to meet people. These changes took control out of hand s and this I regret. I can say however that I have had a happy life and met a lot of fine people.

A: *Thanks for allowing me to talk to you about your life in Crieff.*

Interview held in 1998.

Chapter 14

A Victorian Adventurer

Some years ago, I received a telephone call from Norrie Bull, a local hotelier telling me that he had staying with him a lady from the exotic island of Hawaii. Sanna Saks Deutsch was the Registrar of the Honolulu Academy of Arts. As an amateur historian with a specific interest in Crieff and Strathearn, it was not unusual to be phoned up with a request to attempt to answer someone's problems from the past. This request was however more than a little unusual. Ms. Deutsch it turned out was seeking information on one Constance Frederika Constance Gordon Cumming who had lived for a time in what is now the Tower Hotel at the top end of East High Street in Crieff.

Who was this lady with the obviously aristocratic name and what was she doing here? The Tower Hotel forms part of what has been known for long enough as College Buildings. Built by a Dr Malcolm at the end of the 18th century they have had a varied and chequered career over the span of their 200 year existence. Constructed to house medical students it comprised the main central building with wings off on either side and a walled garden to the rear. With its panoramic views over the Strath towards the distant Ochils, it must have proved quite conducive to the academic labours of its young occupants. With the death of the Doctor the buildings were split up into rooms for sixteen families of weavers. Cotton weaving was a most important aspect in the economic prosperity of Crieff and this end of the town contained many engaged in the trade. It was a "cottage" industry with many members involved. The father operated the hand loom whilst in many cases his wife worked as a "winder". The balls of cotton were woven into striped and checked ginghams sent to Glasgow and exported abroad.

With the eventual decline in manufactured cotton around the time of the American Civil War, the weavers made way for a strange mixture of the local police force and the Episcopalian inhabitants of the town! The cells were on the ground floors and the basement whilst the upper apartments became a school for about 50 children during the week and a centre of worship on Sundays. The Episcopal vicar eventually resigned his charge, bought the buildings, ejected the inhabitants carried out extensive alterations and opened it as St. Margaret's College for Young Ladies. His pupils came from near and far including the south of England. The education offered was

Malcolm's or College Buildings located at the top end of East High Street, Crieff, have had a multitude of uses over the last two centuries and a fascinating history.

equally cosmopolitan with four resident governesses, two English, one French and one German. In addition music and drawing masters came twice a week from Glasgow and Edinburgh, travelling by rail to Greenloaning and thence by coach to Crieff, returning the next day to the cities. Despite the excellence of the College, it was destined to end in a sad and tragic manner. Crieff at this time had no proper water supply, the drinking water coming from a number of wells throughout the town. The College without effective sanitary arrangements was vulnerable to a variety of diseases such as measles, scarlet fever and whooping cough. Some thirteen years after its foundation a virulent outbreak of typhoid hit the school resulting in the death of two students and the French governess. The end was indeed nigh! Students were withdrawn and it was found out that the finances of the establishment were in a hopeless muddle.

Before long the proprietor sold up and the buildings changed hands a number of times, reverting eventually to small flats and the main building was a private residence let as lodgings. It was at this time in the history of College Buildings that Constance Gordon Cummings enters the scene. Born into one of Scotland's oldest families, her father was chief of the Clan Cumming descendants of the Comyns who were at one time Earls of Buchan, Earls of Menteith, Lords of Galloway and Lords of Lochaber. A descendant of the Red Comyn who was the one stabbed so passionately by Robert the Bruce in Greyfriars Church in Dumfries.

The family owned tracts of land throughout the north east as well as a number of country houses including Gordonstoun later to become a well known public school. Eka, as she was known to the family, was the daughter of Sir William Gordon Cumming and his wife Eliza Maria Campbell of Islay and Shawfield. What then was Eka doing in Crieff so far from her family base?

The answer makes a fascinating tale. Born in 1837, she was 14 years old when she visited the Great Crystal Palace Exhibition in Hyde Park with her father. As one of 13 children her family life was one of excitement. Her older brother Roualeyn for whom she seemed to have a particularly special affection was a famed big game hunter of his time and Eka took great delight in reading his diaries with their descriptive accounts of life in the heart of the African jungle. Indeed as soon as she was old enough she set off for India and the Himalayas, crossing overland between Alexandria and Suez (the canal had still to be built) on the way and sailing across the Indian Ocean to the sub continent Eka was but 21 years old!

An accomplished writer as well as a painter, she filled her diaries with a wide selection of tales. Her sketch books depicted a world she had only read about and such was her will for accuracy that with her she took a large zinc block on which she etched. This was the start of her insatiable thirst for travel. She spent her years travelling and pursuing her passion for adventure and the unknown. She visited China where she worked with the blind and wrote a book on Chinese typing, Japan, India, Ceylon (or Sri Lanka as it is now known), Fiji, Africa, Hawaii and the United States where she crossed the plains in a covered wagon! Amongst her acquaintances were General and Mrs Ulysses S Grant of Civil War fame.

It was becoming clear why the Curator of the Honolulu Art Gallery was interested in Eka! She had spent quite some time on the islands and in that period had painted pictures of the colourful volcanoes as well as writing yet another book. Indeed her artistic works are still greatly revered by the peoples of Hawaii and that was the reason for Ms Deutch's mission to Crieff! She was trying to locate more of her paintings here on Eka's native soil! A quite remarkable lady of her time!

Chapter 15

The Architecture and Buildings of Strathearn
Past and Present

Crieff

I can recall reading in a potted history of the Strath published some years back where it stated quite categorically that the *"19th century architecture is not one of Crieff's outstanding assets and that there is not much to see in the way of antiquities except for a very worn market cross under a canopy."* This somewhat dismissive rejection of the town's assets and attractions is considered ill balanced and not at all reflective of Crieff and indeed Strathearn's many hidden gems.

Crieff, the "Capital of Strathearn" reflects little of its dynamic past. A past filled with Highland caterans and their black cattle, industrious weavers and active resistance to the delay in the enfranchisement of the workers and of course the Jacobite presence in the Strath which succeeded so aptly in putting the noses of the Calvinistic Presbyterian "meenisters" out of joint with their espousement not only of Epicopalianism but of, say it softly, the "auld faith"!

We do however digress when it is our intent to highlight some of the architectural "gems" missed by the aforementioned historian! Crieff itself is made such an attractive place by its mellow brown sandstone worked from the many quarries around the town. Sadly time has taken its toll and the soft nature of the stone with its propensity for severe exfoliation or flaking of the many layers does not augur well for the future. One trusts that the protective rendering carried out in recent years does not destroy too much the rich character of the original material.

The attraction of Crieff is its townscape rather than particular buildings. The higgledy pigledy variance in storey height, the differences in roof pitch, the often out of keeping addenda to older fabric, all go to make it visually attractive. If you look at the main thoroughfare, the East High Street, High Street and West High Street central axis, one realises that there is virtually no building line! The bumps and protrusions would give modern planners palpitations! A glance back at the original plans of central Crieff starting with Woods map of 1822 and the subsequent Ordnance Survey publications graphically illustrate the reasons for the current attractive hotch pot! Coming in from Perth, the stagecoach driver would have had to rein as approached what is now the "Pret" or Pretoria Bar at the corner of Mitchell Street or as it was called then "Water Wynd". For about one hundred yards westwards the road narrowed with long demolished buildings jutting out into the main road. Whilst the 19th century builders took cognisance of the needs of the then highway traffic, the Post Office and other newer properties on the south side still were built somewhat too close to their northern neighbours thus exacerbating the congestion of the present age!

The old Crieff flour mill now replaced by the Park Manor flats.

The long gone handloom weavers of the town have left their mark in many parts of the Town. In the early 19th century some 40% of the work force were engaged in some form of cloth production as weavers, spinners, hecklers, tambourineers and a variety of other trades which have long since slipped into oblivion. The handloom weavers worked out of their own homes, a truly cottage industry. Good examples may still be seen on the upper part of Mitchell Street, on the north side of Millar Street and on Hill Street (or Hill Wynd as was known at the time). These cottages were mostly single storey with steep roof pitches. The weaving shed was often situated to the rear or as in the case of the Burrell street houses in the attic space. A wander down Drummawhandie from Burrell Square reveals a remnant of this vibrant past. The first house on the left hand side shows examples of gable windows which at one time threw much needed light onto the shuttles and pirns of the spinners and weavers.

Census analysis of Crieff from 1841 onwards allows us to plot were about these weavers actually dwelt. East High Street was a part of the town where the click of their shuttle could be heard. The distinctive College (or Malcolm's) Buildings, now sub divided into flats and the Tower Hotel housed some 16 families of hand loom weavers whilst if you turn down Ramsay Street beside the now semi derelict Crown Hotel you are in a part of the town that was virtually all involved with linen and cotton production. Known as Brown's Lane, the small cul de sac to the east of the ancient St Thomas's Well now named Alma Villa and Alma Place (after a Crimean War battle) was aptly named Shuttle Close and prior to its demolition in the mid nineteenth century had a somewhat unsavoury reputation as a place where the lower strata of Crieff society hung around.

Close by the Cross of Crieff lies St Michaels Parish Kirk. The Cross itself is now housed in the old Crieff Prison below the Tourist Board Office in what was the Town House. The building now functions as the Community Hall, having been sold for a nominal amount by the Trustees of the Church of Scotland to a group representing the citizens of Crieff. Built in 1787 it can be described as being in the traditional style with a castellated tower built off the south gable. Sadly it has suffered the ravages of time and the original sandstone has been harled over in drab roughcast obscuring any embellishments that may originally enhanced the building. The slates have been replaced with utilitarian asbestos cement tiles currently covered with a heavy moss growth. Most of the smaller panes of glass in the tower windows have been smashed enhancing the general air of decrepitude that sadly pervades this once important part of the town's heritage. This building replaced an earlier structure on the same site which to quote the little booklet published in 1982. *"The old church, a Gothic building, 95 feet long and only 18 feet wide was too small for the Parish. Very little is known about previous buildings. Dr Cunningham, speaking at a dinner in connection with the laying of the foundation stone of the Strathearn Terrace Church, made this interesting comment: 'Previous to 1787 an older Church stood here surrounded by the graves of former generations. How far back the Church goes I do not know; probably to the time of the Reformation. Most of the Churches of the Reformation were poor structures – some thatched with heather. Probably there was an edifice on this spot for 800 or 1000 years.' While the Church was being erected, services were held in a tent. When the Church was partially built, with the roof completed and seats in the gallery, there was heavy shower, and so the congregation adjourned to the Church, probably to get away from the thunderous noise of the rain on the canvas. When the contractor heard of it, he seized the opportunity to stop his work, as he realised his estimate of £705 5s 10d had been to low. It is said that the building was not finished for 40 years. The feuars erected a few pews, but the majority of worshippers sat on the stools, stones or turfs. Adequate seating was only finished in 1827 at the joint expense of the heritors and feuars. There was accommodation for 996 persons allowing 18" to each member! The feuars let as many seats as they did not require at between two and five shillings. There were no free seats for the poor, except as few gifted by Lady Baird Preston of Ferntower, in a day when there were many poor people in Crieff, who had to resort to begging.*

They were relegated to temporary stools in the passages. When the old Church was demolished, 40 gold coins of Robert the Bruce were found in a wall, perhaps to secure them from possible raids by Highlanders They probably passed into the possession of some of the neighbouring gentry."

The graveyard surrounding the old Kirk was "tidied up" by the Local Authority about 1995. Regrettably, there seems to have been little empathy with the past. Whilst the grassy sward that surrounds the old building undoubtedly makes it easier for motorised mowers and facilitates general tidiness, little thought seems to have been given to the worthy citizens of our ancient town. I receive regular enquiries from all the airts regarding ancestors buried in the old Kirkyard. Sadly many of the stones have gone. The tidy arrangement of many of the remaining belies the fact that many of the original stones have "disappeared" and the growing number of people searching out the past will be disappointed by their visit to the Old Kirkyard. Fortunately a detailed survey of this and other Strathearn burial grounds was made back in 1972 by Margaret Mitchell and published by the Scottish Genealogical Society. Copies of the *Crieff* and other transcriptions are held in the Family History Department of the County Library, The A K Bell, in Perth. Tucked away in the south east corner of the burial ground lie the remains of the Parish Clerk's house and the village school. Access to the church was from Pudding Lane (now Bank Street) and not the present one off Church Street or the Kirkgate as it was known at the time. The new Parish Church was constructed in Strathearn Terrace (formerly George Street) and opened for worship in 1882. Perusal of the columns of the Strathearn Herald of the period makes interesting reading. The ceremony of laying the foundation stone was performed by Dr Porteous of Croftweit with Masonic ritual to the fore. A procession had made its way from the Mason's Hall in Comrie Street to the site of the church led in style by bands and much pageantry, reminiscent no doubt of the Michaelmas Fair held regularly in the town until the demise of the weaving fraternity in the mid 1800s. George Murray Porteous was perhaps the town's most eminent citizen of the time. Born in October 1816 in Gavelmore Street in Crieff, he was a graduate in medicine of Edinburgh University although in the 1881 Census it stated that he was not practising. He made his money in Calcutta in India where his wife Delia and his daughter Helen had been born. According to his son, his fortune was made from the manufacture of sulphuric acid or vitriol. He also claimed that his father had in fact discovered chloroform despite the widely held belief that it was in fact James Young Simpson. The 1881 Census records him living at "Springbank, Croftweit" which was a large Georgian house at the junction of Mitchell Street and Strathearn Terrace opposite the site of the new Parish Kirk. It was demolished about 1990 to make way for the sheltered housing of Strathearn Court. His son Alexander was the author of what is oft regarded as the "bible" of the Town's past, Porteous's *The History of Crieff* published in 1912. The elder of the two was undoubtedly a man of substance having donated the cost of the church tower as well as erecting the hall which bears his name. A feature of the new St Michaels are the two elegant pillar lamps, designed by the eminent architect Sir Gilbert Scott RSA, which were erected on either side the main entrance.

Lost Gems

Sadly the passage of time has seen many of the Strath's unique buildings disappear from our ken. Not all succumbed to the ravages of time. Some

Rhuad Mhor, the shooting lodge of the Murrays of Ochtertyre pictured some years before it disappeared under the waters of the enlarged Loch Turret.

were "terminated" when it was adjudged that they stood in the way of progress. Into this category comes Rhued Moihr (sic) the turreted shooting lodge of the Murrays of Ochtertyre. The creation of an enlarged Loch Turret in the 1950s to provide a bountiful water supply for the Central Belt saw the demise of what was a most attractive building in the true vernacular. It now lies under the water at the far end of the Loch and even in the driest summers is unlikely to reappear. The 1860 *Tourist Guide to The Beauties of Upper Strathearn* republished by Alan Colquhoun in the 1990s has a delightful etching of the Lodge complete with crow stepped gables, smoking lums and a Victorian "Miss Ballantyne", split cane rod and the attendant ghillie!

In these savage, liquid plains,
Only known to wandring swains
Where the mossy rivulet strays

Far from human haunts and ways;
All on nature you depend
And life's poor season peaceful spend.

Since the last War, we have lost three stately homes all in the vicinity of Crieff. What Hitler's bombers failed to achieve, neglect, dilapidations and ever increasing upkeep and repair bills accomplished within the space of a few years. Ferntower House commanded a prime position above what is now Crieff Golf Course. Once the home of Sir David Baird, the hero of Seringapatam and a contemporary of the redoubtable Duke of Wellington (*see Chapter 12*), Ferntower was sold off by auction in 1911. At that time, Edwardian Britain was at its prime, little aware that the clouds of war were on the horizon. Ferntower was a very desirable Estate. The house itself according to the sales brochure contained an entrance hall, dining room, double drawing room, two sitting rooms, twelve bedrooms, two dressing rooms and ample servants' accommodation. Prospective purchasers were advised that it was lighted throughout with gas, and it has also an excellent supply of water from the town of Crieff. Apart from the mansion house, there were extensive stabling and offices described as being *"commodious and suitable for horses and motors with two Coach Houses, one Harness Room, ten Stalls, two Loose Boxes and ample accommodation for Coachmen and grooms"*. The Garden extended to 3.75 acres with a further 2 acres of flower garden whilst the rest of the 170 acres of policies (now the Golf Course) were guarded by a high wall and four lodge houses which still remain. The Edwardian Estate Agent waxes lyrical when he goes onto to describe these grounds as being intersected by tastefully formed Avenues and walks and studded with stately trees. Although primarily agricultural, the shootings on the Estate in the period 1910/1911 would have had present day conservationists leaping about in rage. Apart from 2 roe deer, 6 grouse, 387 partridges and 171 pheasants, the list showed that 10 capercailzies and 21 golden plovers met their fate although in a greener mood, marksmen claimed some 1409 rabbits.

Ferntower had been in the possession of the Campbell Preston family. In 1810 Ann Campbell Preston married General Sir David Baird. The distinguished artist, Raeburn painted the 53 year old soldier and his newly acquired bride. At the time of the sale of the Estate in 1911, Dr TH Meikle who had established the Strathearn Hydropathic in 1868 was the tenant of Ferntower House at an annual rental of two hundred and fifty pounds per annum, a not inconsiderable sum in those days. Baird and his wife had extended the house moving in, in 1814. The appended picture (page 103) shows what was in all probability the final appearance. The original mansion was that lower building to the right which is in the traditional Palladian style of a Scottish Gentleman's House of the 18th Century and bears a similarity in certain aspects to the better known Glendoik also in Perthshire.

Sadly, time caught up with Ferntower and in the 1950s, the Army were called in to blow up the decaying shell. The adjoining stable block remained and up until the 1980s at least two of the flats were occupied. Of the sylvan walks where Davy Baird enjoyed his well deserved solitude, the trees have long since gone. The gardens and policies have given way to the well-cut fairways and close cut greens of Crieff Golf Course which give constant pleasure to the worthy citizens of Crieff and the many visitors to the town pitting their skills against the intricacies of the most excellent Ferntower and Dornoch courses. I am sure the Bairds looking down from their celestial platform whole heartedly endorse these modern changes!

Inchbrakie House, home of the Graemes of Inchbrakie,
another gem now lost.

Other "lost" dwellings of distinction that have been disappeared include the mansion of Inchbrakie, once home of the Graeme family. In Chapter 10, I recounted the tale of the witch of Monzie and the ultimate demise of the family's estate of Inchbrakie. The first Graeme of Inchbrakie was a son of the first Earl of Montrose and founder of the (Perthshire) Kincardine branch of the clan. His father gave him a charter to it as well as land at Aberuthven, dated June 1513. He married Margaret Stewart, granddaughter of the Duke of Albany, a brother of James IV of Scotland.

The fifth Graeme of Inchbrakie was Patrick, cousin of the celebrated Marquis of Montrose. During the turbulent Civil War period in our history, the family were strongly supportive of the Stewart cause. He received the Marquis at his House of Tullybelton (in the nearby parish of Auchtergaven) when he arrived in disguise from England. Graeme conducted his cousin

Abercairney House, admired by Queen Victoria, but sadly no more.

to Blair Atholl where he raised the Stewart standard. Perhaps for this allegiance and his subsequent major part in the contretemps that followed (including of course the bloody events of Tibbermore), the family of Inchbrakie were made to suffer. What is not generally known is that Cromwell burned down the original Castle of Inchbrakie and imprisoned Patrick on a charge of "outlawry". He was released only on Earl of Tullibardine and Lord Drummond signing a bail bond for him. The site of the original Castle lay close to the demolished mansion. To quote from Marshall's *Historic Scenes of Perthshire* (Oliphant and Co, Edinburgh, 1880) *"The site of the Castle which Cromwell gave to the flames, may still be traced. It had been a strong family fortress, surrounded by a moat, and defended by a draw-bridge. The present House is close by where the old Castle stood; and the old yew tree in the Park still survives. It is said to be the largest of its kind in Scotland; and the tradition has it, that its thick foliage was once for a time the hiding place of the great Marquis of Montrose."*

Patrick Graeme had a grandson who came to distinction in the ecclesiastical world. After being an officer in the army of James II, he took himself off to France where he became a monk of the Mendicant Order of Capuchins at Boulogne. It is said that he took the vows of the cloth as a form of penance for killing a friend in a duel. He died as Superior of the Convent of Boulogne. According to the Statistical Account, there was a portrait of him at Abercairney Abbey in his Capuchin dress and another at Inchbrakie together with a family tree which he had drawn, exhibiting his pedigree for several generations.

One cannot conclude a piece on lost treasures without mentioning the mansion of Abercairney (see page 125), demolished comparatively recently falling victim to high remedial costs and its oversize for this modern age. The house was visited by Queen Victoria and Albert in 1842 during their stay at Drummond Castle. To quote Marshall once again, "*Major Moray – Stirling and the Hon. Mrs Douglas received the Royal visitors at Abercairney. They alighted and went through the chief apartments of the House. They were in rapture, as they might well be, with the elegance of the mansion, and the splendour of its furnishings, and, above all, with the beauty and loveliness with which nature and art had surrounded it ... It may be truly affirmed, we believe, that they saw nothing to surpass it, and little to equal it, in several points of view, in that memorable visit to Scotland.*" Sadly, it is no more.

Chapter 16

Fowlis and its changes

A comparison between 1793 and 1844

The village and Parish of Fowlis Wester has been something of a microcosm of the past. The new building of the 1990s and subsequently has perhaps destroyed this uniqueness. Gone is the life that made this small village and Parish that little bit different. It is a village that, sadly, is somewhat neglected in the visitations of tourists to Strathearn. Fowlis breathes history – it is unique. I choose to compare the Statistical Accounts of 1793 and 1844 to help illustrate how things have changed.

PARISH OF FOWLIS WESTER
FROM THE STATISTICAL ACCOUNT
PUBLISHED C 1793 AND WRITTEN BY
THE REV MR STIRLING, MINISTER OF CRIEFF

The Parish may take its name from the estate of Foulis one of the principal baronies of which it is composed. The Parish and estate receive frequently the additional title of Wester to distinguish them from the Parish and estate Of Foulis Easter also in Perthshire but on the confines of Angus. Both these estates are now the property of Sir William Murray of Ochtertyre. The latter however was not long since a part of the estate of Gray, and the former was more anciently part of the Earldom of Strathearn; but six or seven centuries ago both were in all probability the property of some person of the name of Fowlis who gave his family name to his lands. The first of that name in Scotland is said to have come from France in the reign of Malcolm Canmore; and branches of that family became proprietors of extensive baronies in different counties of Scotland, which from them still retain the name Foulis. The word seems to be derived from the French feuilles that is leaves; to which the three bay leaves worn by persons of the name Foulis on their arms apparently allude .The name names of most places in this part of the country being evidently of Gaelic derivation, some have imagined Foulis to be derived from the two Gaelic words fou lios, that is, below the orchard. There is not however the smallest vestige of any orchard near the village, much less in the grounds above it; and had the name been formed from the words now mentioned it would probably have been accented on the last syllable, whereas the letter "i" is not heard in the common pronunciation than the final "e" in the word feuilles.

This Parish lies in the north side of Strathearn having that of Crieff on the W; Monzie NW; Little Dunkeld N; Moneidie NE; Methven E; and on the S, Madderty, from which is separated by the Pow excepting about 40 acres of Madderty which are on the north side of that river. Fowlis is eight miles long and six broad. The great road from Perth to Crieff an extent of 18 miles, enters it on east side, ten miles from the former of these towns, and leaves its western extremity within two miles of the latter.

FACE OF THE COUNTRY

The soil in general is red clay or till which on some of the best cultivated farms becomes blackish and loamy by plenty of good manure. The soil is considerably deeper in the south than in the north side of then Parish. A high ridge running from east to west along the top of what is called the Braes of Foulis divides it nearly into two equal parts. The lands on the south side of that ridge are by far the most valuable and generally the best cultivated. The church stands in the centre of this district and contiguous to it is the village, containing 44 families, who are all lodged in poor, low, thatched cottages, excepting the parochial school master and principal inn keeper who have each a house, two stories high, covered with blue slate. The village can hardly be expected to emerge from its obscurity, since the great road which passed through it is now removed to the lower grounds, half a mile southward. On the declivity of the high rising lands, 400 yards west of the church, stands the manse, which presents a very extensive prospect to the south, east and west and, surrounded with wide, unenclosed sloping fields of moderate fertility, looks down on the richer plains below, as well as on an agreeable variety of grown trees, young plantations and gentlemen's seats, which, so far as they respect this parish shall be noticed afterwards. There is not a sixth part of the parish inclosed. Stripes of coppice wood, in which ash, and especially oak and birch are prevalent. These with the additions more lately made may extend to 16 acres. The hills or moors on both sides of the Almond contain several tracts of black moss which supply most of the people with their principal fuel; but the more industrious tenants in the south part of the Parish, use few peats except in drying their corns for the mill, choosing rather to carry coals from Blairngoine which is twenty miles distant. The usual cart load is 30 tons, tron weight; this they purchase at 1s.1/2 d. The same quantity of English or other imported coal at Perth would cost 3s., otherwise the easy carriage thence would command preference.

HERITORS

The number of heritors with names and comparative worth of their estates within the Parish, will appear from a view of their valued rents here subjoined.

Heritors	Estates	Val. Rent
Moray of Abercarney	Abercairney	£3026
Moncrieff of Moncrieff, bart	Gorthy	£1598
Murray of Ochtertyre, bart	Foulis Wester	£1500
Smith, Lord Methven	Keillar	£1270
Drummond of Logie Almond	Logie	£549
Maxton of Cultoquhey	Cultoquhey	£362
Robertson of Lawers		£118
Grame of Inchbrakie	Pitnaclerach	£83

The whole valued rent is £8506 Scots. The real rent will amount to £4000 and is paid with the price of near 6000 bolls of oat meal and barley, annually exported to Perth, Crieff and the Highlands.

The first of these heritors is patron of the Parish and his principal seat in it. The house of Abercarney having received various additions in different ages, as fancy suggested or convenience required, is less remarkable for the elegance of its architecture, and diversify the than for the very extensive and complete accommodation which it affords: But the numerous fenced fields, gardens, and plantations around it, excite equally the ideas of richness and beauty. The imagination is exceedingly delighted with the approach devised by the present proprietor, while, after passing for 500 yards through a large plantation, along the side of a deep den, in which a considerable stream appears, through the over shadowing trees and shrubs with which its steeps are plentifully stored, and then retiring obliquely 300 yards farther under a shady grove, it presents in succession to the view, the wide sloping lawns, the venerable oaks, the pleasing cascades and fanciful lakes which adorn scene.

NB Some 150 years after this was written the house was demolished to be replaced with a modern structure where the family still live.

Near two miles to the north west of this ancient mansion is the house of Cultoquhey, the seat of the only other resident heritor, which, with the delightful adjoining wood, struck the eye of every traveller with peculiar pleasure, while the public road lay about 800 yards distant to the south. But since the highway has been conducted by the north side of the house, these beautiful objects appear with less advantage.

NB Again since this was written Cultoquhey {pronounced Cult-y-whey} was demolished and replaced by a somewhat stern building around 1820. It included a small chapel and was the seat of the Maxton(e) Graham family. The Maxtones married into the neighbouring Graham of Inchbrakie family hence the double barrelled name. The original Maxtone estate was sold of bit by bit eventually becoming a hotel around 1960. There have been a couple of fires which damaged the fabric but restoration was carried out and the is now under Italian ownership. The Treviso Rugby Club stayed there in 1997 when over here to play the Caledonian Reds in a European Cup match.

POPULATION

By Dr Webster's list in 1755, the population was rated at 1,706. In 1770 the number of souls was about 1,100. In 1794, the souls now are 1,224. Males are 608, females are 616 and there are about 40 births annually and 25 burials. Among the head of families are

Butchers	2
Fiddlers	2
Inn keepers	5
Shop keepers	7
Shoemakers	9
Smiths	9
Wrights	10
Taylors	10
Weavers	50
Farmers	106
Besides small farmers	63

The tradesmen do not fully supply the parish with the commodities in which they deal. The weavers however, beside the linen and coarse woollen stuffs they made for the inhabitants, began a few years ago, to be much employed in working scrims, a thin narrow linen for the Glasgow market. This manufacture ceased all at once about June 1794 on the capture of some of the West Indian Islands and the speculation thereby excited among the Glasgow traders.

FARMERS, AGRICULTURE

(**NB** This is a brief extract from the original documentation)

Of the farmers, three have sheep farms: The largest of these contains 1300 acres, feeds 600 sheep and yields £75 of yearly rent. The sheep are of the black faced Linton breed and of a small size.

Those in the preceding article styled small farmers are such as cannot yoke a plough without the aid of their neighbours and generally pay under £1 each for their possessions, which rarely exceed 8 or 10 acres. That is commonly tradesmen or work with a horse in buying and carrying meal, yarn and other commodities.

Perhaps the best managed farms are such as extend from 120 to 200 acres. On one of 150 may be kept eight work horses, three or four young ones and between 40 and 50 black cattle, old and young. Four draught horses were yoked to a plough 20 years ago but two horse ploughs now almost universally prevail. A farm of this size requires four men, two boys and two female servants. The years fee of a principal manservant is £10; that of an inferior man £7 or £8; to boys from £1 to £3; a female servants from £2.10/- or £3 with the produce of a lippie of linseed sown. A considerable number of additional servants is necessary in harvest.

Many farmers have what are called cottars to whom they give a cottage and a small garden, with sometimes an acre of land and a cows grass for which the cottar pays £3 or £4 he has two acres and ten shillings more if his land is ploughed by the tenant. But no cottar gets any land except on condition of working with the farmer for reasonable wages whenever required especially in harvest.

Such a farmer's family as that now described feed chiefly on oatmeal, barley meal, potatoes, milk and cheese. What animal food they use is from Michaelmass to Whitsunday and consists one bullock salted for winter beef, one hog in spring and between 20 and 24 quarters of mutton purchased occasionally through the year. Though the tenants are decently clothed and their circumstances upon the whole tolerably easy and more plentiful than formerly; yet they are far from being affluent or in a situation that raises them above the necessity of manual labour.

QUARRIES

On the Cultoquhey estate is a quarry of the best stone for pavement in all the country.

POOR, RELIGION, CHARACTER

The people are in general devout as well as sober and industrious, lovers of peace and well affected to government.

The inhabitants of the northern half of the parish commonly use among themselves the Gaelic tongue; all of them however can speak English, which is the only language spoken or understood on the south side of the hill. Though there are no remarkable instances of longevity, yet the people in general are abundantly healthy. Consumption sometimes occurs, and the jaundice has been more frequent of late than ever known; but agues which were prevalent 20 years ago have, for a long while, disappeared.

There is at Fowlis on the 6th of November annually, a market for black cattle. About 1000 may be presented for sale and a third part of them supposed ready for slaughter.

STATISTICAL ACCOUNT PARISH OF FOWLIS WESTER 1844 WRITTEN BY THE REV. ALEXANDER MAXTONE, MINISTER

NB This was the second Account written some 50 years later and reflects the changes in the village and parish. The following are the relevant extracts.

The village of Fowlis was once a place of considerable importance where the Stewart

Fowlis Wester of yesteryear showing the Fowlis Inn, now a private residence
and the original Pictish symbol stone now located in the adjoining kirk.
A facsimile stands on the original site.

*of Strathearn held his court. This court is memorable for one decision at which Sir
Alexander Moray of Abercairney who had been charged with culpable homicide pled
in 1397 the privilege of the law of the Clan MacDuff and being with the ninth degree
of consanguinity to him he was acquitted.*

*Montrose first erected his standard in the parish at the bridge of Buchanty where he
was joined by the Drummonds and the Graemes.*

*Andrew and George Moray of Abercairney and Peter Maxtone of Cultoquhey were
slain in the fatal field of Flodden in 1513. A proprietor of the latter house has been
long famed for a celebrated litany, which he repeated every morning at a well near
his residence. Anthony, of the same family, was, in the reign of Charles I, Prebendary
of Durham.*

*Mr Drummond of Broich was deposed from his office of Minister of Fowlis at the
revolution because, as stated in the records of the kirk session he would not pray
for King William and Queen Mary.*

*The earliest entry in the parochial registers is in 1674. They are voluminous and
regularly kept with the exception of a few years after the Revolution.*

*In the village of Fowlis, there is an ancient Calvary cross on one side of which is
a representation of a wolf chase, in bas relief, in which there are figures of men on*

horse back and a blood hound. The wolf appears grasping a head in his fierce jaws and tradition says that in the course of the chase, he ran through the town of Foulis and snatched off the head of a boy. In the same group of figures are six men dressed in a peculiar grotesque style and following an animal, supposed to be led to the sacrifice.

The only other heritor resident in the parish is Maxtone of Cultoquhey, whose property has been in the singular predicament during all the time it has been possessed by his family, of being neither increased nor diminished. He has the same common ancestor with the Maxwells, the one being Maccuston, a Saxon and the other Maccus villa, a Norman termination, denoting the town and villa of Maccus, the son of Undyn, who had lands upon the Tweed, which acquired from him the appropriate name of Maxton and Maxwell.

Fowlis appears to have been a favourite seat of the Druids. Several of their clachans have been demolished but there are still four large Druidic stones standing west to the village one of which is a cromleach or alter stone in which there is an artificial cavity where the blood oil of the sacrifices flowed. On the summit of the hill due north from the same place, there is a Druidic circle of stones and a double concentric circle. This is believed to have been the temple of an Arch Druid which when erected was probably in the midst of a forest in which were the oak and a consecrated grove, the favourite objects of their superstition. The circle consists of sixteen stones between which and the double circle there is a large stone incumbent, where the arch Druid stood. To the west of the temple there is a siuns which signifies in Gaelic a mount of peace, near which is a fairy hillock where urns have been found and which was believed to have been inhabited by an inferior kind of genii called fairies. On the siuns the Druids held assizes when it was customary to kindle a large bonfire called Samhinor the fire of peace. On Hallow eve, a Druuidical festival, these fires are still lighted up, in this district, and retain the same name.

NB The above account seems somewhat coloured by Victorian mysticism regarding the Druids and what they were. Later research identifies the Strathearn area as being the Pictish Kingdom of Forten. It was they who ruled the area up until the arrival of the Romans. The high ground above the village where the stone circle is, commands a superb view over the Strath and, similar to Stonehenge in the south of England was the centre of worship at the summer solstice. The circle is similar to the one about a mile away at Monzie. They date further back however than the symbol stone and are Iron Age (2000 BC).

The fact that in the 1840s fires were being lit up at the time of the old Celtic festivals indicates that the old superstitions prevailed in places like Fowlis for well over a 1000 years after the arrival of Christianity. In Jackson' book *The Symbol Stones of Scotland* he wrote (page 130) "Magical properties are attributed to the stones and various practices grew up, but whether they had any connection with the original custom it is hard to know: for example the Class ll stone at Fowlis Wester was rubbed all over with animal grease annually until the turn of the last century!"

The mansion house of Cultoquhey has also been lately erected. It is a structure of beautiful and substantial workmanship and graceful proportion in the style of an Elizabethan age, from a design of Mr Smirke.

The population has fluctuated considerably. In 1831 it was 1,681. This fluctuation owing to the erection of the village of Gilmerton to the quoad sacra part of the parish being included in the census and to the extent of modern farms. The population of the villages is 396 and the country 1285. Average births are 30 annually, deaths 26 and marriages 18.

NB A quoad sacra parish was one created for ecclesiastical purposes and was a sub division of the civil parish although the boundaries may not always coincide.

The principal manufacture in the parish is the weaving of cotton cloth and the weavers are furnished with the raw material from Glasgow. The construction of sieves, a species of handicraft is almost peculiar to this place. Several families have been for generations employed in this trade.

The town and lands of Lacock adjoining Fowlis are a burgh of barony with the privileges of a weekly market every Wednesday, and two yearly fairs; but none of these have been held of late.

There are two villages in the Parish, Gilmerton and Fowlis. The latter generally is in the state in which it has been for centuries and in its exterior appearance is a monument of the building of olden times. The progress of improvement however has commenced. Several of the houses have been lately slated and the inn has been rebuilt in a substantial and commodious manner which with the school house is an ornament to the village.

There are four schools in the parish.

St Methvanmas market is held at Fowlis annually on the 6th of November and is a useful market for the sale of black cattle and hiring servants. This was anciently the festival of the parish and the anniversary of the saint to whom the church was dedicated at its consecration, when the people constructed pavilions and booths to indulge in hospitality and mirth, which also became a commercial mart and assumed the name of feriae or holyday.

Both these reports are plucked from the past. They perhaps indicate the changes that abound in society and indeed how in comparative periods things change quite perceptibly.

Chapter 17

Notes and Traditions of Balloch

NB: This was described in *Crieff: Its Traditions and Characters* by D. Macara {Edinburgh, 1881}.

The beautiful valley of Balloch lies about three miles westward from Crieff. The Loch is half a mile in circumference and seem as if set in a basin. From its west margin rises the deer forest of Torleom to a height of 1400 feet, finely wooded and well stocked with deer. On the north are the steep slopes of Knockmawhinner and the Whitedrums. On the south are the famed forest terraces of Drummond, with the castle crowning the height, and on the east is an opening down into Strathearn. A century ago {**NB:** circa 1770 – CM} some hundred families lived in the quiet retirement of this sequestered spot, snugly sheltered from the rude blasts which shook the surrounding districts . At that time the loch was much larger than at present, and a great undertaking by the Earl of Perth was the cutting of the den to drain off the loch. This improvement brought numerous workmen from great distances, a few of whom settled in the locality, and became the progenitors of many denizens living in the Strath. Artificers expert in their occupations were scarce, and in 1762 the Commissioners of the Forfeited Estates, of which Drummond or the Perth Estate was one, advertised for weavers, wheelwrights, blacksmiths, masons, etc., to settle at Crieff, when feus and other suitable encouragements are to be given to such artificers if found duly qualified. A number did settle down on the Estate, and a detachment of old soldiers was located in the field of Bennybeg, which so far accounts for the multiplicity of surnames in the district. In the days of James IV, the Clan McRobbie inhabited Balloch, and rendered the Drummonds signal service on the adjoining height at the battle of Knock Mary, where both defeated the Murrays. The Drummonds granted the McRobbies an aisle in Muthill Church for the burial of their slain, which right is still held by the chief of the clan, and a document in connection therewith was produced in 1826, when the dispute was brought up regarding the right to erect an Episcopal Church on the old site of the Muthill Parish Church. In the beginning of the century the ruins of an old castle were distinctly visible in the field adjoining the east side of the loch, but to whom it originally belonged, or who owned it, is unknown. Latterly, tradition says that it was occupied by the Lairds of Balloch, the last of whom died in lodgings many years ago. It is reported of him that, trying to vie with the neighbouring family of Perth, he got into debt, and his creditor took possession of the estate, and so the laird had to shift his quarters. A story is told of him in his latter days, when getting his porridge one morning, his land lady remarked that they were "gey an' thin". "They have a worse fault than that", said the Laird; "they are few of them." At that period there were numerous small lairdships owned by the Drummonds surrounding Drummond Castle, such as the Drummonds of Concraig, Pitkellony, Strageath, etc, but all merged into one.

A number of years ago, when cutting oak copse, the work people found flint arrowheads in the neighbourhood of the old castle. As noticed, some 100 families lived and moved in the vicinity of the loch. About the commencement of this century they were reduced to 70. Father McDonald, the priest, who died forty years ago, lived on the west of the loch, and had his primitive thatched small cell or chapel behind the house. His room is still intact. The system of cottaring, or a large farm being sub-divided to cottars, was greatly in fashion, and often the occupier of the farm more than paid his rent by his drawings from these cottars. A number of these cottars lived in the vicinity of the loch, and it was customary when the harvest was over, and the stacks secured under "thatch and rope", for a cottar to employ a bagpiper to play his wildest music for an evening round the stacks so as to frighten the rats to the other side of the loch. The valley had its quota of tailor's, hecklers, lint-millers, dyers, wrights, thatchers, and broguers. The last representative of the latter was George Tainsh, who in his early days was a broguer in Balloch, and made and mended for the late Lady Willoughby. He removed to Crieff, where he pursued his calling of shoemaker to an old age. His firmly knit body, although of stature small, was well known in all the market stances of the surrounding market towns and villages. He never wore a neck cloth or a buttoned shirt-collar, disdaining the enervating habits of his neighbours. He scarcely had an ailment, and when he had a cold he washed it off by copious draughts of spring water.

The Howe of Balloch was famed for its witches, who had an abominable fashion of turning themselves into black cats. The last reported cantrip by one of the fraternity happened about forty years ago at a displenishing sale at Newbigging, when the reputed witch was caught milking one of the cows, causing the milk to pass through a charmed ring, with a view to take the milkness from all the other cows to the one she proposed buying. She was unceremoniously turned out. Rowan tree branches were fastened at the byre doors to prevent witches from having any influence on the cows, and a horse shoe which had been lost from a horse's foot was by the fortunate finder nailed inside the door for luck. Fairies and brownies roamed at their own sweet will, and death raps and other signals, along with "dead candles", foretold the decease of neighbours. Large numbers of wild cats, foxes, polecats, and other wild animals prowled in the neighbourhood, and all kinds of hawks were so numerous that a person had to remain beside the chickens when being fed out of doors to prevent their winged enemies from carrying them off.

Shortly after Lord Willoughby came to Drummond Castle – about seventy years ago – he caused frequent raids to be made on the wild cats, and by ingenious traps placed on the dykes; he soon made these pests scarce. His lordship also introduced the rearing of pheasants brought from England. The young ones were fed for some time on ants brought from Torleum, and thereafter allowed to haunt the woods. The rearing of young rabbits was for a time carried to a great extent, and a view of the myriads that thronged the fields was one of the sights of the locality, more especially when the dogs were sent to chase them up the slopes. At that time boars were introduced into the forest, and hunting them was sometimes indulged in; but one day one of the hunters having got isolated from the rest, a boar attacked him, and he narrowly escaped with his life. This put an end to the sport, and the dangerous animals were disposed of. The Hill of Torleom was previous to this mostly bare of firs and larches, and the junipers and blaeberries grew and throve to an astonishing extent, so much so that the inhabitants of the surrounding districts annually made excursions for the purpose of bringing home the large and luscious berries of the famous hill. After the wood was planted the berries degenerated, and few if any are now found to be there. The top of Torleum is the weather-glass of the surrounding parishes. According to the appearance and movement of the mist or cap which often rests on the top of the hill are the prognostications of the weather. The following rhyme regarding it has long been familiar:

On Torleum tap there is a mist

And in the mist there is a kist
And in the kist there is a cap
And in the cap there is a drap
Coup up the cap, and leave the drap on Torleom tap

The Strath has produced a sprinkling of great men, but we believe that the following will be new to most readers. The truth of the story was duly vouched for by the late intelligent tenant of Broadlea, Mr James Miller. About the middle of the last century a hedger named Bayne, and his family, lived in the Balloch. Having a strong leaning to the Duke of Perth and Prince Charlie, and having seen the last of the '45, resolved to seek a home in another land, and with this intent he and his family and others set sail for France. A storm came on, and they were driven on Corsica, where they were hospitably received, and were known as Bayne, or Buon and his party. In course of time his sons were called Buon- de- parte, or Buonaparte, and who now figures in the history of the world as the great Napoleon. Hurrah for Balloch!

Chapter 18

The Good Old Days !!

Some extracts from past periodicals reflecting life in the 18th and 19th centuries

Examination of the files of some of the Strath's old newspapers and other archives of the time reveal an interesting picture of the changing social and economic patterns in the area. The first extract shows that justice was far from tolerant of miscreants and that banishment to the Colonies was still in vogue!

Crieff Herald, April 1857

Alexander McGregor, from Perth Prison, charged with theft by means of house breaking; in so far as, on the night of 28th February last, he entered an out house in Auchterarder, belonging to Lewis Anderson, and stole two ferrets, which he afterwards sold in Crieff. He pled not guilty but was found guilty and sentenced to four years penal servitude.

The problems with the demise in hand loom weaving as detailed elsewhere in this book manifested itself in the Minutes of the Crieff Weavers Society. As can be seen the apparent euphoria at the satisfactory state of the Society in 1851 is in sharp contrast with the announcement six years later of its termination.

The Perthshire Courier, 12th June 1851

Crieff Weavers Friendly Society: The AGM of this Society was held on Wednesday the 4th curt. It is generally understood among the members that the deacon is to leave for Glasgow to commence business there; a very full attendance was the consequence. After calculating the income and expenditure for the past year, a balance remained in the Treasurer's hands of twenty-five pounds five shillings and seven pence. It is gratifying to see a Friendly Society in so prosperous condition after 83 years existence. The Society took this opportunity of recording the highest sense of worth of their late deacon, Mr John Selkirk and a vote of thanks was unanimously tendered him by the meeting for the unwearied zeal and ability he has displayed over 4 years and trust he will succeed as well in his new vocation as his high moral character and abilities entitle him.

The Crieff Herald and Strathearn Advertiser, 28th March 1857

Crieff Weavers Friendly Society: This Society was dissolved on Monday last. The house property of the society was disposed of last summer and the funds arising from that and other sources amounted to nearly five hundred pounds. This sum was distributed amongst the members in proportion to the length of time during which each had been connected with the society in shares ranging from ten shillings up to seven pounds ten shillings. These dividends have come very opportune to many poor persons in this inclement and dear season. As usual on such occasions there are a good many disputes some of which may require legal proceedings before they are rectified and there have been rather too many instances in which the dividend has proved but a questionable benefit.

Strathearn was fortunate that although hand loom weaving struggled on for longer than elsewhere in Scotland, its eventual total collapse was offset by a number of other factors which helped both unemployment and the local economy. This extract from 1860 showed that many weavers were turning their hands to jobs in construction. The arrival of the railway gave jobs not only during the construction stage but also in the general complex infrastructure of the Companies involved therein. Porters, way leave men, signal men, station masters were in demand whilst the goods sidings, saw mills and cattle pens all required men and women to carry out day to day tasks. The railways of course brought people to live in the Strath and as we can see from this report on housing in Auchterarder the start of the Victorian moves back to the country towns had begun.

The Perthshire Courier, 22nd November 1860

Auchterarder: Property is rising in value here, feus in some parts of the village with houses erected on them which use to sell a few years ago at a good deal under one hundred pounds have of late brought nearly two hundred and from the scarcity of accommodation house proprietors are reaping a harvest in the shape increasing rents which in some cases have advanced from 40 % to upwards of 100%. The Commissioners of the Common are however to feu on a pretty extensive scale in a short time. The improvements on the Common Muir are now being prosecuted with great energy. There are upwards of 100 men employed at present and more will soon be added. A number of weavers have commenced the work in consequence of their usual avocation being in a languid state.

Prior to this however, the construction of more substantial commercial and residential properties had already begun to get under way. Indeed the number of Georgian buildings in and around the Strath is probable greater than many might suppose. Woods map of Crieff dated 1822, shows the development undertaken along Commissioner Street in what were described then as the Old and New Feus. The Commissioner Street name is historically interesting. Crieff despite the assertions of its anti Jacobite Presbyterian "meenesters" in the aftermath of the "burnings" of Strathearn villages after the 1714 Uprising, was still Drummond country and, per se, presumably offered a threat to its Hanoverian masters. The Government set up under an Act of 1752 a provision to annexe to the Crown, estates of individuals who had come out in the '45. These annexed estates such as those of the Strathearn Earls of Perth who were traditional Jacobites, fell under the direct control of Commissioners, hence Commissioner Street in Crieff!

Georgian architecture is attractive and well thought out. Burrell Square, or the Octagon is it was originally known is a classic example of a terrace of this period and has a distinction which sets it apart. The tollhouses that were constructed to implement the Turnpike Acts are still with us in many cases. The renovated building at the junction of Dollerie Terrace and the Perth Road in Crieff is a fine example whilst the somewhat eccentric Little Culdees in Muthill, built with stones from the old Culdees Castle exemplifies ambition brought about by the growing affluence of many of the populace. There was a desire to escape from the confines of the traditional thatched biggin. Indeed the transformation from thatch to slate as a roofing material is emphasised by this extract from an advert for a "roup" (auction) in a local paper of 1809.

The Perthshire Courier, Monday 28th August, 1809

To be let by roup for 3 years: A slate quarry having formerly been worked upon the Hill ground of Drumdevore and there being favoured appearances of slate in several places of the hill grounds above Ochtertyre which if opened and properly worked would afford a much more convenient supply of slate for Crieff and neighbourhood than is now derived from the more distant slate quarries of Aberuchill, Glenartney, Glenalmond or Glenshee.

Sir Patrick R Murray will grant by Public Roup a lease of 3 years of the former slate quarries and of those quarries which may be discovered and worked upon his estates of Ochtertyre, Monzievaird and Callender. The Roup will take place at Drumdevore on Monday, 11th day of September at 12 o'clock precisely.

Ochtertyre, August 18th, 1809.

The Cattle of the Tryst (Published in 1811)

In 1811, MacDonald's general view of the agriculture of the Hebrides was published in which it described Highland cattle as being mainly of the Kyloe breed and being middle sized, capable of being fattened to 50 stone (c. 320 kilograms). Their colour is black, dark or reddish brown. The hair should be glossy thick and vigorous. The three types of cattle found in the west Highlands are the Kyloe, west Highland or Hebridean.

These beasts are a small breed. They are hardy and light with the ability to cross soft ground and bogs. They are referred to as bullocks or stotts. In 1798, the native breed of Argyll is now much greater in size than that found on the Island of Skye. These beasts are short in the legs, round in the body, straight in the back and long in the snout. They are described as being black, dun, branded and brown. Black is the most common colour. These beasts weigh 360 to 400 lbs when sold at age 3 to 4. They can be brought up to 560 lbs and over when pastured in England.

Elsewhere we have discussed the radicalism of the hand loom weavers in Scotland. Those in Strathearn played their part in the quest for a more liberal enfranchisement albeit in a non-violent way, restricting protest to marches, parades and speeches with the emphasis on debate rather than violent protest. There is little doubt that the authorities were in a panic. Unemployment and falling wages after the Napoleonic Wars posted warning signs, which for a long while went unheeded. The following on the periphery of Strathearn did not go unheeded locally. "The Battle of Bonnymuir" on the hills above Bonnybridge was in fact an ambush by the Militia on a group of weavers supposedly heading for the Carron Iron Works where the Carronades (naval guns) were manufactured.

Political unrest in Scotland

Perthshire Courier, 1820

On Tuesday the 4th current, information was received at Ayr that on Monday upwards of 60 men had marched from the town of Stewarton in military order to a field in the neighbourhood, for the purpose of drilling, where they remained about one hour; that this party was headed by William Orr, shoemaker in Stewarton, who took his post at the head of them with drawn sword, and gave the word of command; and that John Crawford a Weaver acted as drummer: The Sheriff Substitute and Fiscal, instantly proceeded to Stewarton, and took a precognition, and ascertained fact of these persons guilt, and issued the necessary warrant; but they had absconded the night before. On the 5th of April, William Dunlop and Robert Pinkerton, two of the people who went and were drilled, were apprehended and brought to Ayr, under an escort of the Ayrshire Cavalry, and put in prison (Ayr Courier).

Six coaches have just arrived (three clock) at the new jail, Calton Hill from Newhaven with eighteen prisoners from Stirling Castle. They were brought down in the steamboat under a guard of the 4th veteran battalion and a number of police officers.

Lord Elcho's troop of Mid Lothian Yeomanry quartered at Bathgate, received orders at one o'clock on Wednesday morning to proceed from thence to Falkirk; we understand they have since moved forward to Glasgow. Captain Walker and Capt Inglis's troops marched from mid Calder to Bathgate on the same morning. The Musselburgh and Dalkeith troop still remain here, but expects orders to march today, in consequence of the approaching election of Peers. About 60 carronades, and a considerable quantity of ammunition were brought from Carron and landed at Leith Fort.

Yesterday morning, at three o'clock, Captain Brown, with a strong party of police set off in 16 coaches for Glasgow, to aid the civil and military power in the city.

Execution of the political martyrs Hardie and Baird

Perthshire Courier, September 15, 1820

Stirling, Sept 8, half past 7, p.m. – The preparations for the execution of these unfortunate men having been completed the previous night, this morning the scaffold appeared into the view of the inhabitants. On each side of the scaffold was placed a coffin, at the head of which was a tub filled with sawdust, destined to receive the head; to the side of the tub was affixed a block.

The clergymen of the town (the Reverend Drs Wright and Small) and the Reverend Mr Bruce throughout the confinement of the prisoners were unremitting in their duties. The morning previous to the execution was spent almost solely in devotion and reflections suited almost solely in devotion to the awful situation of the prisoners. About 11 o'clock a troop of the 7th Dragoon Guards arrived from Falkirk, and were assisted by the 15th Foot quartered in the Castle.

At a quarter after one the procession left the Castle, and was seen to move slowly down Broad Street, the unfortunate men in a huddle, their backs to the horse, and the headsman with his axe sitting as to face them. They were respectably dressed in black with weepers. The procession was attended by the Sheriff-depute and his substitute, and the Magistrates, all with their staves of office. The troops lined the streets so as to permit the whole to pass slowly and undisturbed to the spot intended for the execution. During the procession the prisoners sang a hymn, in which they were joined by the multitude.

At twenty minutes to two o'clock the hurdle arrived at the Courthouse. Hardie at first ascended followed by Baird and then the headsman. Hardie by mistake was conducted into the waiting room; he bowed twice respectfully to the gentleman who were present. The reverend Dr Wright accompanied Hardie; the Reverend Dr Small and Mr Bruce were with Baird. Hardie turned round, and observing how few persons were present; said to one of the clergymen, "is this all that is to be present?"

Dr Wright read the whole of the 51st psalm; he then delivered a most impressive prayer, after which a few verses of the same psalm, from the 7th verse, were sung by the prisoners and other persons present, Hardie giving out two lines at a time, in a clear and distinct voice, and sung the same without any tremulency.

The Reverend Dr Small then delivered a prayer remarkable for zeal and fervour; after which the 103rd psalm was sung, Hardie giving out two lines at time as before.

The conduct of these men while in the Courtroom was most calm and unassuming. Both, and particularly Hardie, seemed less affected by their situation than any other present; his hand while he held his book, never trembled. Some refreshment being offered, Hardie took a glass of sherry, and Baird a glass of port. Hardie said something, the exact import of which we could not collect. He begged the Sheriff to express their gratitude to General Graham, Major Peddie and the public authorities, for their humanity and attention; he then bowed to the other persons present, and drank off the whole of the contents of the glass. Baird then addressed himself to the Sheriff, and begged to convey sentiments of a similar nature.

On their arrival at the scaffold, there was a dead silence. After a few moments, Baird addressed the crowd in a very low voice. He adverted to the circumstance in which he was placed, and said he had little top say, but that he never gave his assent to anything inconsistent with truth and justice. He the recommended the Bible, and peaceful conduct to his hearers. Hardie then addressed the crowd. He commenced with the word "Countrymen". At something which he said, but which we could not completely catch, and which we must not guess at, there was a huzzaing, and marks of approbation. After a few moments silence, as if recollecting that he had excited feelings inconsistent with his situation he spoke again. He advised the crowd not to think of them, but to attend to their Bibles and recommended it to them, in place of going to public houses, to drink to the memory of Baird and Hardie, that they would retire to their devotions.

After the ropes were adjusted, a most warm and affecting prayer was delivered by the Rev Mr Bruce. At eleven minutes before three, the necessary arrangements being made, Hardie gave the signal, when they were launched into eternity.

After hanging half an hour they were cut down and placed upon the coffins, with their necks upon a block; the headsman came forward, he was a little man; he wore a black crape over his face, and a thick gown. On his appearance there was a cry of murder. He struck the neck of Hardie thrice before it was severed; then held it up with both hands, saying, "This is the head of a traitor." He severed the head of Baird at two blows, held it up in the same manner, and used the same words. The coffins were then removed, and the crowd peaceably dispersed.

Footnote: The execution of Andrew Hardie and John Baird for their part in the "radical uprising" or the "Battle of Bonnymuir" of 1820 took place in Stirling some 20 miles or so south of Strathearn. It was the last execution for "high treason" in Scotland and was a particularly brutal business. The Government were in a panic after Peterloo and feared an uprising similar to that which had occurred over the Channel. The local Militias played their part in the repression of the "radical war" as it became known. The Chartists fight for reform paid off when the Reform Bill became law in 1832. King William granted a posthumous pardon to Hardie and Baird.

By the late 19th century, many of the traditional markets held in the small villages in the Strath were no longer. This *Strathearn Herald* account of the 1882 Turret market near Crieff is typical. Although produce and animals were bought and sold, it was primarily a "feeing" or hiring market where farmers could contract to hire labour for a given period, in the case of the Turret Market, until the Martinmass quarter day. The "halflins" referred to were farm boys.

The Strathearn Herald, 19th June, 1882

This once large hiring market, extending over two days which has become a mere shadow of itself was held on Tuesday last. There was but a meagre attendance of farmers and others. The number of servants inquiring after places were few – particularly women. The engagements made were very much at the same rate as last year. Women were hired for five pounds ten shillings to eight pounds ten shillings to Martinmass; girls and boys, from three pounds to five pounds; ploughman for twelve to fourteen pounds; and halflins from seven pounds to nine pounds. There were few pigs in the market, which sold at from eighteen shillings to twenty shillings.

Highland games are now a popular adjunct to a town's tourist attractions. Highland games now feature abroad where Scots participate in events both sporting and cultural.

Despite the assumption held by many that the "games" were an ancient tradition, the truth is that Highland Games are really a 19th century reincarnation of a much earlier tradition quashed in the aftermath of the last Jacobite Uprising. One of the oldest games was that of St Fillans at the end of Loch Earn which started in 1818. By then the tartan had been rehabilitated in the eyes of the British establishment. Sir Walter Scott and his stage managing of the arrival at Leith of the obese George IV complete with pink tights beneath his kilt, had done what Charlie, the not so bonny prince, had failed to achieve. The gaedhealteachd or Gaelic culture was now the "in thing"! The Scottish upper classes could now parade themselves in front of their bekilted tenantry in what was to become one of the social events of the year! Indeed the social significance of events such as the St Fillans Games becomes quite apparent after reading this descriptive article in the PC!

The Perthshire Courier, August 1829

St Fillans Games: The Eleventh Annual Meeting of the St Fillans Highland Society was held on the 28th ult. on the usual beautiful picturesque arena at the eastern extremity of Loch Earn. They are always looked forward to with much pleasure, by all classes of society in their immediate vicinity, and generally attract a considerable number of nobility and gentry from different parts of the kingdom. On this occasion there was every reason to expect the assemblage of spectators would be very great but owing to several untoward circumstances, these expectations were unluckily disappointed. In consequence of the death of Sir David Baird of Ferntower, a gloom was cast over the surrounding district of country; and a stop was put to preparations which were making for a splendid ball at Crieff. The funeral of this gallant officer being fixed for the same day, on which the games were to have been celebrated, rendered it necessary to postpone them from Thursday to the Friday. In the circumstances several of the nobility and ladies and gentlemen of the surrounding country did not attend the meeting. The weather for some days previous had been also unfavourable, though Friday itself was upon the whole a good day. The sports commenced before two o'clock, but the spectacle did not exhibit the same interesting appearance which it used to on former occasions. At eleven o'clock, the Chieftain with a party dressed in the full Highland garb arrived and after a balloting for new members took place in the Society's Hall and the other arrangements for the amusements of the day were made, the members marched in regular procession, to the ground appropriated for the games. And after an exceedingly well contested competition, which, from the excellent arrangements made, gave the highest satisfaction, the following prizes were delivered, after suitable addresses to the successful candidates, viz:

Pipers – 1st prize to Donald McInnes from Lochaber – a handsome full mounted pipe with silver inscription, presented by the Chieftain. 2nd prize to John McDonald from Fortingal – a handsome silver mounted dirk. 3rd prize to Adam McPherson, piper to the Stirling and Bannockburn Caledonian Society – silver broach.

Dancing – 1st to Peter McLaren, piper, Lochearnhead – a set of sword belts. 2nd to Duncan Menzies, piper, from Glen Lyon – a pair of stocking hose.

Throwing the hammer – 1st to William Drysdale from Crieff – a handsome purse or sporran mollach. 2nd to John McDougal from Foss – a pair of stocking hose.

Putting the stone – 1st to William Drysdale from Crieff – handsome silver mounted snuff mill. 2nd – to John McDougal from Foss – a silver broach.

Tossing the bar – To William Drysdale from Crieff – a handsome pair of silver buckles.

Best dressed Highlander – Hugh McVean, from Crieff – a handsome powder horn, given by the Chieftain.

Boat race – To John McNab, from Callander – a splendid silver quaich.

After the prizes were delivered, the members of the Society adjourned to the hall to elect the office-bearers &c. for the ensuing year, when Lord Willoughby de Eresby was unanimously chosen Chieftain, and McPherson of Cluny, Moray of Abercairney, Sir John Ogilvie, Bart. and Captain William Stewart, Murthly, Vice Chieftains. Stewart, younger of Ardvorlich, was re-elected Secretary, and the other office bearers to remain in office as formerly. After the business of the day was concluded, the Chieftain, and a numerous party, sat down to an excellent dinner prepared by Mr Stewart of St Fillans Inn, and spent the evening with the greatest *harmony and conviviality. In proposing "Prosperity to the St Fillans Society", the Chieftain stated that he was happy to inform the company that it was the intention of the members and patrons of this interesting institution, to render it still more useful and worthy of the patronage and support of the country by combining with its present laudable objects, a school for the instruction of the destitute poor – which was received with applause.*

Hanky Panky at Badin Kittoch!

Kirk Session Records for Crieff February 1707

Not all the information concerning individuals and places of yesteryear are found in the old newspapers. A veritable treasure chest are the old Kirk Session Records. One must appreciate that in 18th and indeed 19th century Scotland, the Kirk was a most dominant force in maintaining a modicum of decorum in most parishes not least of all Crieff! The following is perhaps the equivalent of *News of the World* "exclusive" at a time when most Scots were trying to come to terms with the much-opposed Treaty of Union with Big Brother to the south!

__January 12th 1707:__ The Session being informed of Helen Robin, servetrix to John Lawson in Dallerie, her repairing under sickness to Duncan Leitch in Badin Kittoch, for a charme; Appoints them also to be summoned against Sabbath next.

__February 16th, 1707:__ Helen Robin being summoned and called, compeared, and being interrogated if she under sickness repaired to Duncan Leitch for a cure, answered – she did. Being interrogated what cure he applied or pretended, answered – that he stroked her side with his hand. She being enquired at if she perceived the said Duncan utter or mutter any word the time he was stroking her side, before or after denied the same. Duncan Leitch being cited, called, and compearing, confessed that he stroked her side, and likewise acknowledged that he used some words in the doing thereof. He being desired to express the words, refused to do it, but condescended to tell them sometime privately to the Minister. It being asked why he would not tell them before the session, gave no reason. He being, moreover, asked if he thought there were any virtue in these words, answered – he knew not. He being allowed to against the minister, with the words against next Sabbath, replied – I never spake them on a Sabbath-day. All which the Session considering, are of judgement that the words are a spell.

__1707, Feb. 23.__ – The Minister reports that Duncan Leitch told him the words, but thinking it needless to repeat them to the session, for although there be no evil in the words themselves, yet, in his opinion, they ceased not to be a charm, as the Session had before concluded. They appoint the said Duncan and Helen Robin to be cited against Sabbath next.

__Att. Crieff, March 2, 1707.__ – The officer reports that Duncan Leitch, by reason of sickness, is not in a capacity to attend the session. Helen Robin being summoned and called, compeared, and being interrogated if she went to Duncan Leitch when she laboured under indisposition of body with a design to be charmed, or if ever she heard that the said Duncan used to charme, and withall being seriously dealt with to be ingenuous; she denied that she went with him to be charmed, or that she ever heard of his charming. She being posed with what she was reported to have said as she came from Duncan Leitch, viz., that our forefathers used it, and whatever ill was in it we might use too, since we got good by it, denied that she ever spoke so. The Session refers the whole business to the Presbytery for advice, and recommends to the minister to represent the same.

1707, March 16. – The minister reports that he consulted the Presbytery anent Duncan Leitch, his affair, but the said Duncan now being dead, he thought it needless to communicate their advice. As to Helen Robin, in regard the Session is suspicious of her disingenuity, and that there is no appearance of any probation that she went to Duncan Leitch with a design to be charmed, they appoint her to be summoned against Sabbath next to be informed of the evil of a charm, and in case she hath been guilty, she may forbear the like afterward.

Scotsman, 10th October 1891

The Kind Gallows of Crieff: At a meeting of Crieff Town Council yesterday a very interesting relic of other years was formally handed over to the Town Council for safe custody, this being two parts of the famous "kind gallows"of Crieff, so well known as being referred to by Sir Walter Scott in his **Waverley** and also mentioned by Lord Macaulay in his **History of England** *(sic!!)*. During the great fairs held in Crieff prior to the establishment of the Falkirk Trysts about the year 1770, hanging of cattle stealers was very common, and the Earls of Strathearn and other feudal superiors were wont to hold frequent courts in a field known as the "Stayt". The principal highway in the valley of the Earn led east and west past the Gallows Hill a small knoll nearly a mile from the Stayt. This place of execution is now embraced in Crieff and is at present indicated by a tree, the locality being known as Gallow'ha. Raiders on cattle and sheep caught red handed were disposed of very summarily.

Macauley when referring to these times in his **History**, says: "One day many square miles of pasture land were swept bare by armed plunderers from the hills. Another day a score of plaids dangled in a row on the gallows of Crieff." Sir Walter Scott visited the locality more than once, and most likely he inspected the famous instrument. The last authenticated trial which took place in the Steward of Strathearn's Court is that of the Rev. Richard Duncan, Minister of Trinity Gask (some five miles from Crieff) for the murdering of his illegitimate child. He was condemned and executed on the chief gallows in June 1682. In all probability the gallows were in use up till the time of the Uprising in 1745. The hangman held office till 1746. The timber of the old gallows was for a time kept in a smithy house near the top of King Street and in 1832 a box was made from part of it and sent to Sir Walter Scott. In more recent times it was much cut up and made into "souvenirs of Crieff". Since then the famous relic has passed through the hands of various *owners until yesterday when, as above stated, it was consigned to the custody of the Crieff Town Council.*

Crieff's Burgh Seal

I don't expect many current residents of the town have a vague idea what the ancient seal of Crieff looked like. But again being a resident of Perth and Kinross Council doesn't quite inspire the intimacy of local traditions!

ARMS OF CRIEFF

The above is a representation of the seal that was adopted by the Town Council of Crieff and was duly described in a publication of 1893.

"The seal is emblematic of historic scenes in the district. In pre-historic times the Earls of Strathearn – scions of the Royal family – had their stronghold or castle sit-

uated on Tomachastel, a conical hill some three miles west of Crieff, and on which stands Sir David Baird's monument, a conspicuous object in the valley of the Earn. Singularly enough too, the title is still held by one of the Royal Family of Great Britain – the Duke of Connaught and Strathearn. The Earls of Strathearn, who flourished in the twelve and thirteenth centuries, were succeeded by the Stewards of Strathearn, and they held courts in a field about a mile south from the town, now part of the estate of Broich.

Down till about the beginning of the present century (NB the 19th) the "stayt" or "skeat" where the Court was held was about twelve yards in diameter, with the centre raised, on which the Earls or Chief Judges sat. In 1850, the then laird of Broich demolished the "stayt". The seal represents the Earl sitting upon the mound dispensing justice. On his left is the Cross of Crieff, also a pre-historic relic, and, according to Mr T W Hughes, Professor of Geology, Cambridge University, dates not later than the eighth century. In the foreground are the Crieff iron stocks or pillory, which are still seen at the door of the Court House. They are almost the only remains of this kind in the country. In ancient times criminals were wont to suffer punishment in the stocks, the mode being that the delinquents lay on their backs and had their legs securely locked."

Bull fighting in Methven!

The Perthshire Courier **November 3rd, 1814** gives us an insight into what the douce citizens of the village of Methven enjoyed in days gone by. Not for them the ever popular cock fighting or badger baiting that prevailed in other parts of rural Perthshire in the eighteenth century as village past times. The Methvenites showing Iberian tendencies seemed to be into bull fighting as one of their forms of diversion!

"Long ago at the Methven market was the exhibition of a bull-fight. The man who entered the lists was allowed to choose his weapon. On the last exhibition of this kind a stout country lad turned out, and choose for his weapon a slaughter-spade. The unequal contest was not of long of duration; the furious bull gored the unhappy man, and killed him on the spot, while the multitude looked on with the utmost apathy, and thought it, no doubt, fair play. The awful issue of the combat terminated this savage amusement."

Earthquake at Crieff

The Perthshire Courier of **November 1789** reported the following:

Crieff, November 13, 1789. On Thursday last, the 5th current, at six in the evening, a shock of an earthquake was felt by many persons, from a vibration of the ground. Some affirm it rocked their houses and their bottles on the tables and the stoneware in their shelves clashing together. The inhabitants of Bridgend of Crieff were greatly alarmed and ran to the streets. The convulsions continued about two seconds, and eased with a noise resembling carts driving hard. But at Comrie and its neighbourhood eastwards, about five miles west from Crieff, the shocks of the at the same period exceeded all of the kinds they had been in use of sustaining for two months before. The inhabitants retreated to the streets and the fields, and were afraid to return to their beds. So general was the consternation, that even the dogs ran out of the houses, and the poultry flew from their roosts. The shocks as usual there, terminated with an explosion resembling a cannon, or distant grumbling thunder.

The Crieff Masons – *Scotsman* 19th July 1888

Interesting Discovery in a Foundation Stone

At present a portion of the Freemasons' Lodge Crieff is being demolished for the purpose of extending the building, and this week, while workmen were removing part of a wall on a level with the street, they came upon the foundation stone, in a cavity of which was deposited a bottle containing seven coins of the realm, written documents, and newspapers – all of which were in an excellent state of preservation. The coins consisted of a three-shilling piece (or bank token, as some of the coins bear) of date 1815, George III; a ten penny silver piece (Irish), 1813, George III; an eighteen pence piece, 1812, slightly larger than a current shilling; two silver pieces, much worn – one bearing date 1787 (George III) and the other 1758 (George II). There was also a threepenny piece dated 1762 (George III) and one copper coin (a farthing) of date 1744 (George II). The written documents are:- {1} Copy of the Constitution and erection in favour of the Mason Lodge of Crieff granted by John Young, Depute Grand Master of the Free and accepted Masons of the Kingdom of Scotland, with the consent of David Kennedy Esquire, Senior Grand Warden and George Drummond Esquire, Junior Grand Warden and the other brethren of the Grand Lodge, "*upon a petition presented on the eighth day of August 1739, by the most Worshipful and Right Honourable His Grace James Duke of Perth, for himself and in the name of the other Worshipful Brethren of the Masons Lodge kept at Crieff.*"

NB The Masons Hall still stands in Crieff at the junction of Comrie Street and Lodge Brae. Part of the building is now the local library but the masons still meet on a regular basis and must be one of the oldest groups in the town.

Chapter 19

Towns and Villages of Strathearn

Dunning

The village of Dunning, tucked away below the northern slopes of the Ochils, has a peaceful presence and an illustrious past. Like Muthill, Dunning has had a Christian church since early days. The kirk in the village is mentioned in the charter of 1219 as belonging to the Abbey of Inchaffrey. It is reckoned the tower is probably the oldest part of the building having been constructed in the mid 12th century and then a single storey church with chancel and nave was built onto it. It is believed that perhaps there was an older church on the site. This is based on the evidence of the Saxon style older doorway on the north wall. It is dedicated to the 5th century Saint Serf founder of the Monastery at nearby Loch Leven and someone whose name is found in various places throughout the Strath including Monzievaird near Crieff. St Serf seems to have been Dunnings equivalent of the English St George as recounted in the 1880 publication *Historic Scenes of Perthshire* by the Rev William Marshall. Apparently the district around the village was being harassed by a dreadful dragon which devoured both men and cattle and kept the district in continual terror. The bold Serf, armed only with the breastplate of faith attacked the monster in his lair and slew him with a blow of his pastoral staff. In proof of this legend and in memory of this event, the scene to this day is called the Dragon's Den.

Dunning has an active and innovative local history society who have an excellent web-site (http:/www.dunning.mcmail.com/). It is by far the best local history site around covering Strathearn. It is original, informative and splendidly pictorial. The picture of Peter Flockhart, on of the last weavers to ply his trade in the village is outstanding. For such a comparatively small place Dunning wins the history information contest by a mile. If you have a day or two explore around check out the web site and pay it a visit.

In 1895 Dunning had the unique distinction of having a Lady Town Crier. The following article is gleaned from a chronicle of the time.

"The existence of a novelty in the shape of Miss Miller, the bell woman of Dunning, has reached the southern press, and already a London daily is making

151

copy out of it. A comic paper has also seized the opportunity of eulogising in verse on the subject. We can imagine the look of horror which would overspread the features of the subject of the verses if she saw the illustration which last week's Judy depicts as her appearance at the year immediately succeeding her teens. A blushing damsel dressed in the uniform of the ancient town-crier, and with knickers on, too! The following is the letter-press:

The lady Town Crier – in the little Scottish town of Dunning the town crier is a well to do, maiden lady of fifty, named Miller. She rings all the bells with extraordinary vigour (*Daily Paper*).

> *Wherefore, through the streets of Dunning*
> *Clang the bells in tones so stunning;*
> *Why do they in wild variety*
> *Fright the town from its propriety,*
>
> *'Tis because the crier thrifty*
> *Is a spinster aged fifty*
> *She had lovers rich and plenty*
> *When her years were only twenty*
>
> *Here's her picture , most veracious*
> *Oh, how beautiful, how gracious!*
> *She was then as now, Miss Miller;*
> *Then, as now, she saved her "siller",*
>
> *Though she's rich she still is clinging*
> *To her favourite sport of ringing*
> *Bells, which sound with clamour stunning*
> *Through the little streets of Dunning."*

Battle of Duncrub

Duncrub lies to the north of Dunning. It was there in 964/5 that a vicious battle took place between two contestants for the Scottish throne. Duff, the son of Malcolm I claimed the prize on the death of Indulph who had succeeded Malcolm. Not surprisingly the latter's son Culene or Cullen, decided his claim was superior. In the close proximity of Forteviot, the ancient Capital of Fortren and indeed that of the Scotland of Kenneth McAlpin, the battle was waged. Duff was triumphant but his reign was brief. Four and a half years after mounting the throne, he was assassinated at Forres on the Moray Firth.

In a field to the east of the B9141 road stands a stone reputed to be where Doncha, the Abbot of Dunkeld was slain in the battle. Some two miles south of the village on the B934, Yetts O' Muckhart stands another stone which is reputed to be the site of the killing of Dubdon, The Thane of Atholl. It is said that it was here that he was caught in flight from Duncrub and put to death. The field is (or was according to an 19th Century publication) called Thanesfield.

The Rollo Family

Duncrob was the ancestral home of the Rollo family for many generations. The family are of Norman origin with deeper genealogical roots in all probability going further back to the Norse raiders of the eighth century. A Sigurd Rollo was Earl of Shetland and Orkney and his son Einar was one of the Viking leaders who raided the towns and villages of the Scottish east coast. He eventually turned his attention to the northern shores of France and from there sprung the Dukes of Normandy, 1066 and all that. An Erik Rollo was reputed to be the nephew of William the Conqueror and not surprisingly the family were to the forefront in establishing themselves firstly in the south and then here in Scotland. It was Richard Rollo who came with David I when he returned from the English Court to claim his throne.

Robert de Brus, an antecedent of the great man, granted the Rollos a charter around 1141. By the late fourteenth century, the family had well and truly established their Scottish credentials when in 1380; John Rollo or Rollok received a charter for the lands of Duncrub. Their involvement with the Royal family continued through the years and the lands expanded steadily. William Rollo and his son Robert fell on Flodden's field but the Rollos continued to be an influential family in the land. Andrew Rollo married his cousin thus inheriting yet more land whilst his son Peter apart from being the Bishop of Dunkeld found time to a judge in the Court of Session!

They stayed loyal to Charles II during the Civil War and Sir Andrew Rollo became Lord Rollo of Duncrub. Such adherence caused him to fined £1000 by Cromwell but this was certainly no deterrent. Lord Rollo's fifth son Sir William was a general in Montrose's army and played his part in the victory at Inverlochy when Argyll's nose was badly blooded. He received his come uppance however when he was captured at Philiphaugh and was beheaded at Glasgow in 1645.

The military proclivities of the Rollos were borne out in latter years with Rollos fighting with distinction at Dettingen and in the North Americas fighting to gain Canada as a possession for the British Crown and later in India where the seventh Lord Rollo commanded a force of marines. In 1869 the tenth Lord Rollo was created Baron Dunning, a British peerage and a seat in the House of Lords. The family although moved from Duncrub which is now a holiday centre, still live in the Dunning area.

Methven

Although Methven lies well and truly in the heart of Strathearn, its proximity to Perth often causes people to forget that of all the small villages in the area, Methven has a history that extends back into the turbulent past. One of the first mentions is when the Thane of Methven took revenge on Cullen who had been crowned King at nearby Scone in 972. Cullen was by all accounts a pretty unsavoury character having, according to the historians of the period *"abandoned himself to the grossest licentiousness and in a few years had become such an abhorrence to the Nation that a Parliament was summoned to meet at Scone for the purpose of deposing him."* Cadhard, the Thane of Methven's daughter had, according to the story been abused by the King, and he was determined to seek revenge. As Cullen made his way to nearby Methven Castle, the Thane duly accomplished what many others may have wished but were too scared to implement. Cadhard dispatched the King and by all accounts, not many tears were shed around the district. *"This ended the filthy sensualitie of the King; the reproachfull infamie thereof remaineth in memorie with his posteritie, and it is not like to be forgotten whilest the whole world goeth about."*

Methven Wood which lies between Almondbank and Methven Castle is a site of historical import. Wallace is reputed to have sheltered there when spying out the land and the defences of Perth. The Battle of Methven was fought here in 1306, when Bruce was tricked by the Perth based, English "Guardian" of Scotland, one Aymer de Valence, Earl of Pembroke. Bruce had, in the *"chivalrous spirit of the age"*, challenged Pembroke to a dual in open field. The Earl promised to do so next day and so Bruce and his small band retired to the sanctuary of the Wood where the stripped themselves of their armour and went about preparing the evening's meal. Suddenly the English troops rushed out of the undergrowth and despite stout resistance, the Scots were on the occasion outflanked and caught completely short. Bruce himself unseated Pembroke but was himself unhorsed in the heat of the moment. When Edward of England heard the news, he ordered Pembroke to immediately execute the prisoners. The Earl for what reason we cannot be sure decided to release Randolph, Bruce's right hand man, ransom some of the other more important prisoners and hang and quarter the remainder *"in a spirit of merciless revenge"*.

Methven Castle stands in a proud position overlooking the Strath and has after a number of years of neglect been restored to something of its original splendour thanks to the Murdoch family who are the present custodians. The first known occupants were the Mowbray family who were Norman in ancestry and arrived in Scotland in the 12th century. Indeed it was one Sir Philip Mowbray who enjoined with the English visitors at the Battle of Methven to eliminate Bruce as he began his crusade to recover much of occupied Scotland. His brother Robert was granted Methven as part of his reward for supporting the English cause. After the Wars of Independence when Bruce triumphed Mowbray who was at this time Governor of Stirling

Castle was forced to hand over, nay surrender, the fortress to the triumphant King of the Scots. The penalty was the loss of his Methven Estate and Bruce bestowed the lands on his son in law Walter, Lord High Steward of Scotland.